Take Your Money
And Run!

Take Your Money
And Run!

ALEX DOULIS

ECW PRESS

Published by ECW PRESS
2120 Queen Street East, Suite 200, Toronto, Ontario, Canada M4E 1E2

LIBRARY AND ARCHIVES CANADA CATALOGUING IN PUBLICATION

Doulis, Alex
Take your money and run! / Alex Doulis.

ISBN-13: 978-1-55022-771-0
ISBN-10: 1-55022-771-8

1. Finance, Personal—Canada. 2. Tax planning—Canada—Popular works.
3. Income tax—Canada—Popular works. 4. Retirement—Canada—Planning.
I. Title.

HG179.D68 2007   332.024   C2006-906634-5

Cover and text design: Tania Craan
Production: Mary Bowness
Printing: Transcontinental

This book is set in AGaramond

With the publication of *Take Your Money and Run!* ECW PRESS acknowledges the
generous financial support of the Government of Canada through the Book Publishing
Industry Development Program (BPIDP).   Canadä

DISTRIBUTION

CANADA: Jaguar Book Group, 100 Armstrong Ave., Georgetown, ON L7G 5S4

PRINTED AND BOUND IN CANADA

ECW PRESS
ecwpress.com

CONTENTS

The first edition of this book was published in 1994. The previous decade had been a barn burner for the politicians, bureaucrats and all the hangers on. It was a time of innovation. Art Eggleton was promoted to the Senate as a result of initiating the trouble-free payoff for ex-mistresses by sending them to the Immigration Review Board. Gib Parent, Speaker of the House, after having lost custody of the wife's airline pass, took to having his girlfriend ferried to Ottawa from Toronto in a Parliamentary limousine at the taxpayers' expense, thus increasing employment for displaced Toronto taxi drivers. But Canadian governments — always forward-looking — were planning even bolder steps. Human Resources was planning for the future arrival of Jane Stewart by devising a method of blowing $3 billion. Guité and Brault were meeting in the fleshpots of Ottawa planning the Adscam debacle. Even the public was engaged in the rip-offs. My firm, Gordon Capital, had purchased a chunk of the future Prime Minister, Jean Chrétien, by paying him $50,000 a year while he was out of office.

The nice thing about all this for Ottawa was that the Canadian taxpayer, the ultimate victim, was powerless to do anything about it. His donation to the rip-off was taken as a source deduction from his income. Once every four years he could go to the polls and elect the next group of scoundrels who always promised that this time they would really end government waste and reduce taxes – even eliminating the GST. Promise anything – you'll never have to deliver. This was proven in the Supreme Court of Canada where a citizens' group took a politician to court saying that he had reneged on a written promise not to raise taxes. You know where judges come from so of course they ruled that a campaign promise written or otherwise was meaningless. Hurray for democracy.

Canada has a progressive tax system which means that if you earned between $10,000 and $20,000 a year, each extra dollar of income you earned cost you sixty cents in lost benefits and increased taxation. If you were billionaires like the Bronfmans, you had a Senator talk to the Minister of Finance to change the rules so as to not pay $700 million in capital gains tax. While being mindful of the tax burden of the opposition's rising star Paul Martin, you have the *Income Tax Act* changed so as to end the need to pay any tax at all on shipping income. Once again Canada had come to the aid of its long-suffering billionaires. Why give them a tax break when you can eliminate their taxes altogether? And there was nothing we could do. Or was there?

At that time spending had gone out of control and there were trial balloons constantly filling the air over Ottawa. Tax large RRSP pools? Tax excessive house prices? I could see myself being carried away on any number of those balloons. There were no trial balloons on spending cuts. So I ran. I became a refugee from confiscatory taxation and four years later I wrote a book about it that became an enormous best-seller.

My wife warned me that publishing a book that allowed Canadians to take their destiny into their own hands could only lead to trouble. Wives are always right and so I became "known to the tax collectors." After having paid all my departure tax they discovered unpaid tax (totally fictitious) after publication of this book. As late as fifteen years later Teri Korz, in CRA's St. Catharine's office, is still trying to collect after having had it explained to her that this was no tax liability — it was a vendetta. Ordinary Canadians regarded me as a hero. After the book was published, I met readers golfing in Ireland, singing cantatas in Switzerland and sailing the Mediterranean, all tax free. Many Canadians take a break from living there and paying its high taxes. Some come back to become Members of Parliament or Prime Minister.

Has anything changed? No. Canadians are still one of the highest taxed people in the world and the poor and the middle class pay most of the taxes.* Can you change the system? No. Therefore if you don't like the rules and you can have no influence on them the answer is to quit playing and paying. That's what I did and this is how I did it. You can do it too.

---

* The government would have you believe that high earners pay the greatest proportion of tax but there are many Canadians with gargantuan incomes who pay little or no taxes because of their tax breaks. Read what the headline says, "Canadians with *reported* incomes over . . ." paid whatever of the total take. How much did the guy who earned $5 million and reported $1,000 pay?

INTRODUCTION

This book is about my good friend Angelo.

Angelo was my bridge opponent for 20 years, and in those years I cannot remember him grumbling about the circumstances in Canada, although I am sure he must have nodded in agreement, on occasion, with those of us who did. Angelo rose in his organization because he always tackled problems as they arose and planned for the difficulties he could foresee. In the end, he was more of a financial wizard than the accountant he was trained to be.

The other bridge players all recognized Angelo's strengths in business because his star kept rising. What we did not know was that he was planning his personal financial life in the same way he husbanded the financial resources of his partners. A short anecdote will give you some insight into the man's mind.

One evening after bridge, he asked one of the players, a geologist, why copper for three-month delivery was usually priced higher than spot (that is, copper for immediate delivery). Jake, the geologist, explained that any commodity for delivery three months in the future had to include in its price the interest cost of the money put toward holding it for three months.* Therefore, the difference in the two prices reflected the interest that a copper buyer would have earned had the money been left in the bank.

I later learned that Angelo had set up a partnership within his organization that took fully hedged positions in commodities (they bought and sold at the same time, but with different delivery dates so as to never actually be at risk of holding material). The difference in pricing, due to timing, was taken into the partnership as capital gains. By a sleight-of-hand, he had changed fully taxed interest into capital gains, which, at the time, were taxed at half rates.

Some years later, Angelo amused us with the story of how a representative from the tax department had come to their office and informed them that he knew what they were up to. They were changing interest income into capital gains. Angelo's organization was a stock-brokerage firm, so there was some justification for them to be trading in commodities. The tax department was not going to allow this to continue and, as their parry, declared Angelo

---

* A rational investor has two options when looking at a commodity investment. He can put the money in the bank and earn three months' interest or put the money into a commodity and earn no interest. To accommodate his lost interest, the investor adds the lost interest to the price of the commodity.

and his partners to be professional traders. They would therefore be ineligible to receive the capital gains treatment for the trading profits. For professionals, the gain from trading is considered business income and taxed at full rates. This is not the end of the story!

With his partners' agreement, Angelo decided to take advantage of the benefits available to them with their new status as professional commodity traders.

The *Income Tax Act* allowed a 3-percent credit to be taken against taxes payable for the value of inventory held at the end of the year by those involved in buying and selling any products, including commodities. Angelo arranged for his partnership to hold a large (again fully hedged and hence riskless) position in copper at year end, for two weeks. Each of the partners would take a pro rata portion of the tax credit against his taxes. This is still not the end of the story!

The tax department sued the partnership for taxes payable to the extent of the inventory tax credits taken. The lawyer for the tax department stood before a judge and explained that the partners had first taken the tax benefits due to amateur traders and then, when they were deemed professionals by the tax department, chose to take the benefits due to professionals. The judge did not wait to hear the defence. He asked the Revenue Canada attorney which category the partners fell into: were they professionals, as declared by Revenue Canada, or were they amateurs? While much muttering went on at Revenue Canada's bench, their spokesman described how, if the defendants were allowed to be classed as amateurs, they would take benefits clearly not intended by the *Income Tax Act*. However, they could not be treated as

professionals, because again they would be reaping benefits. The implication was that the *Income Tax Act* bestowed
only penalties, not benefits. The judge pointed out that
Revenue Canada would have to pursue these men as
either professionals or amateurs since, unlike sports, there
was no "semi-pro" status in the *Income Tax Act*. Revenue
Canada's case was thrown out of court. Of course, they
appealed. They lost that case, too.

So now you know the kind of man you are dealing with
in this book. But what circumstances did Angelo confront
in his own financial planning? He told me about the
warning signs that had led him to abandon the conventional path. He feared for his financial future as long as he
was trapped in one country's currency, in one economy,
where he was powerless to change the circumstances. He
said, "If you can't participate in the control of the game,
don't play."

He told me of the signs that indicated very difficult
times ahead. He observed that elected officials at all levels
were buying their seats by promising ever greater benefits
to the masses, paid for with debt. It started, he said, when
John Diefenbaker promised the fishers unemployment
insurance for the periods they couldn't work, and continues today as farmers are paid for the shortfall in their
expected incomes. Welfare, Angelo said, should apply to
the incapacitated, not to those with thousands or millions
of dollars in assets.

He attributed the Québécois separatist movement not
so much to culture, but to a desire to reassert control over
one's destiny. He concluded that a realignment of Canada
as a federation, with power being removed from the central monolith and its bureaucracy, would mean benefits

for all the citizens of Canada — except the politicians and their minions.

He knew he couldn't change the system. He couldn't use the methods (indexed pensions, tax-free allowances, etc.) that bureaucrats and politicians use to protect themselves from their profligacy, so he chose to escape their clutches.

This is the true story of how he acquired his wealth and held on to it, legally.

CHAPTER 1

Meeting THE SKIPPER

I had received a number of invitations from Angelo and his wife Sarah to come and visit them in Spain during the dreary Canadian winter. Business was slow in the mergers and acquisitions arena, so I decided to take them up on their offer. I managed to find a Toronto-Paris-Barcelona flight.

As I got off the airplane in Barcelona, I thought, this can't be a bad place, it has palm trees. Angelo had instructed me to take the airport train to La Prat and change there for Sitges. Once there, I was to look for him, and he would take me to his yacht, *Amarone.*

How fitting, I thought, that Angelo would name his yacht after his favourite wine. However, I was also curious as to what Angelo would consider a yacht. Looking back on his lifestyle in Toronto, it seemed likely that I should be looking for not much more than 30 feet of boat and, very likely, one of those mass-produced French boats.

The countryside was pleasing enough. From the train window, I could see the beginnings of a vegetable crop. I couldn't tell from the window whether I was looking at lettuce, spinach, or cabbage; in any event, it was all green and growing in November. An odd sight, I thought, when in Toronto the only thing that was growing were the profits at the winter sports suppliers. At this moment, I should have been looking at a new pair of skis and the latest rear-entry, mid-height, foam-filled, three-buckle ski boots with the optional battery pack for heating. However, I had blown the cost of new ski boots on a plane ticket to visit my old bridge opponent, Angelo.

Angelo had surprised us all during one of our weekly bridge games by announcing that we would soon have to look for a new fourth. He was retiring at age 50 to pursue his dream of sailing across the Atlantic to his parents' native Italy. We were all aghast. Angelo had led a quiet life as an accountant at a major brokerage firm. He had lived unostentatiously in the same house in downtown Toronto for some 25 years. We all encouraged him to buy something better. After all, with his position and status as treasurer of his firm and a shareholder of some substance, he could afford at least something in the million-dollar range in Rosedale or Forest Hill. At our weekly bridge games, however, Angelo claimed poverty and said that such opulence was beyond his reach. He continued to walk to work from his downtown renovated row house. His new-found independence was not in keeping with the economic circumstances he had described to us. How in the heck could a 50-year-old man retire and live with any decency? This, I hoped, Angelo would tell me.

Well, he certainly looked different! The grey was gone from his temples. I recognized the trousers he was wearing, as I had seen them last summer when we had him and his wife over for a barbecue. He certainly wasn't filling them now. He looked as if he had shed 50 pounds. As I got off the train, Angelo threw his arms around me in a great bear hug.

"Angelo," I said, "you've lost a lot of weight."

"Stewart, I have lost 40 pounds from my waist, and more from my shoulders, but that's a lot of philosophical stuff you don't want to hear about. What about you?"

"Oh no, I haven't changed — but you sure have."

"Oh, I haven't changed. I've been reborn," he said with a smile.

I thought to myself, Oh no, he's going to give me one of those "evangelical" routines. Warily I said, "How do you mean that, Angelo?"

"Well, I've changed the course of my life. You know that when you leave college, you are born again, because you become a worker, and when you change careers, you can be born again. I chose to be born again at retirement."

"Great, I wanted to ask you about that."

"It can wait until we get to the boat."

We walked down the hill to the yacht basin for Sitges. As we walked along the jetty, I kept looking for what I expected to be Angelo's cramped and uncomfortable sailboat. Finally, we stopped by a 43-foot Hans Christian ketch, upon the stern of which was written the name *Amarone*. I was stunned. Even before stepping aboard I knew it was expensive. I said to Angelo, "This is some bloody boat. What's it worth?"

"About $300,000."

"In real dollars, or Canadian dollarettes, as people call them offshore?"

"Real dollars."

"How can you afford it?"

"Oh, I don't own it. I rent it."

"Wow, it must be expensive."

"Not really, I pay $3,000 a year for it."

"What, you get a boat like this for $250 a month?"

Being an investment banker, I had quickly calculated that, at a 10-percent interest rate, the cost of capital* for this boat would be $30,000 per year, or $2,500 per month. Angelo must have somehow managed to trick someone into renting the boat at one-tenth of its annual capital cost.

"Ang," I said, "how did you manage to get the boat at such a low rental cost? Are the owners crazy? Who are the owners?"

"The boat is owned by a company in the Turks and Caicos Islands that has chosen to rent it to me at a very accommodating rate."

"But why?"

"Well, let's just say I do them favours and they do me favours."

"Do you own this company?"

"Now, Stew, you are asking questions that are neither easy nor beneficial to answer. Why don't you come aboard and we'll have a glass of sherry."

I noticed as we stepped aboard the Hans Christian that she didn't move. Going down the companionway ladder, I could see that the interior was finished in either teak or mahogany. I'm not much on woods, but I knew it looked expensive.

---

* The cost of capital is the rent or interest one must pay for the use of capital to own an asset.

CHAPTER 2

Revelations

·····························

It was a warm November night. Yes, November. Angelo and I were sitting on the deck of *Amarone.* I sat on the propane storage box, and he on the life raft. We were each clutching a glass of sherry in one hand and a Monte Cristo Number 2 in the other. The Monte Cristo Number 2's are those lovely torpedo-shaped cigars that are rolled on the thighs of some sweet, young lovelies in Havana. Here in Spain, they cost $10.50 apiece, about one-quarter of their Toronto price.

I asked Angelo what had happened — an inheritance, a big market score, insider trading, real estate, what?

"No, Stew, my parents are both alive and living within their constrained circumstances, brought on by the past few years of inflation.

"It is hard to make a big 'score' in the stock market and, once having done so, even harder to hold on to it. I must admit, though, that financial markets did pay for my escape from corporate life. As you know, insider trading is illegal, and I am not in jail. As for real estate, only the sales agents make money in that arena.

"I sold everything I owned, cashed in my Registered Retirement Savings Plans (RRSPs), and moved on with my wife, Sarah, to a new life. I could see only diminishing returns from my further participation in the financial markets, and my sons, who had both started university, no longer needed me."

"Angelo, I can't see you selling your property and all. That's scary. Also, didn't you take an income tax beating on the RRSPs?"

"Well, at first, it was scary. I left a comfortable lifestyle where I could assess the risks and measure the rewards. But I knew if I didn't overcome the fear, I would die in the traces or be pensioned off to Florida. I opted for a whole new lifestyle, and fortunately Sarah was willing and eager to try it. Of course, the greatest fear is that you won't have enough money."

"Do you?"

"No, no one ever has enough money in our usual corporate lifestyles because there are always toys out there that we just have to have. Often that need to consume is just a psychological trick we play on ourselves to obtain a reward for our wonderful efforts. Get past the consuming and you have almost enough money. In my new lifestyle, $35,000 a year is ample. But that means no more Dunhill blazers at $1,000 a pop or Guccis at $400 a throw. I don't even have a DVD player.

"The important thing is the budget. Know how much income to expect and then what your costs should be. I figure that to run the boat, feed and clothe us, plus cover all the incidentals, it costs us $95 per day. Our bond interest is almost double that, at $160 per day. Until we experience a year at this and see what our stabilized situation is, I intend to stay at the $95-per-day expenditure rate."

"Wait, when you say your bond interest is $160 per day, is that before or after tax?"

"Well, Stew, they're identical. Our pre-tax earnings equal our after-tax earnings."

"Angelo, are you telling me you don't pay taxes?"

"Yes. In order to escape the system, you have to maximize your earnings. If you assess your current situation, you will find that your highest cost of living is taxes. Eliminate the luxury of taxes and you double your income."

"How does the Canadian government feel about this?"

"Well, I understand that there were audible sighs in the Senate when they learned that I would no longer be subsidizing their indexed pensions, to the extent that some members awoke, and cries of 'unpatriotic' were heard. But in all seriousness, what can they do? I have the money. It's outside Canada. I don't reside in Canada and I don't use their services. To make it worse for Ottawa, it was all arranged by the government's rules and, therefore, is completely legitimate."

"Sure, it may be legal," I said, "but what about the morality of it?"

"Stew, please don't mention government and morality in the same breath. Canada's first prime minister was a drunk who went around asking bagmen for $10,000 cheques. He set the tone for the century to come. Read a book called *A*

History of Canadian Wealth by Gustavus Meyers. You'll find that the country's financial elite descended from bootleggers, con men, and outright thieves.*

"Do you think that they could have amassed their fortunes without the connivance of government? When the 'Home Bank' failed in 1923, did the bigwigs have their money in it? No, they had all withdrawn their funds the week before. Over 70 percent of the companies in the Toronto Stock Exchange's 300 Composite Index are controlled by five families in Canada. Do you think they got there by not using the rules to their advantage? I believe everyone should obey the law, especially when it is to their benefit."

"Okay, let's stick with the legality of it, Angelo. I remember that the *Income Tax Act* says that everybody has to reside somewhere. Where do you reside?"

"Stew, you have hit on one of the important aspects of escape: the other residence."

Of course, I was right; everybody has to live somewhere. But what Angelo had done was very clever.

He found that under Italian law, there was a way he could obtain Italian citizenship. I remembered his giving up lunch get-togethers to go to the Italian consulate and present ever more papers supporting his claim. He told me that, having been told by the Italian authorities that it would take a year to cut through the European-style bureaucracy, he

---

* Gustavus Meyers was an American journalist who hid in Canada in the early 1900s while his life was under threat from New York's Tammany Hall politicians, whom he had exposed for their dishonesty. Meyers' book on Canada was well researched with many references to Royal Commissions, corporate annual reports, and newspaper articles. His book was banned in Canada until 1972. It still can be found in used books stores with ISBN 0-88862-016-0.

budgeted two years for the process. Finally, one summer's day, two years later, he announced proudly that he was now an Italian citizen, as well as being a Canadian.

I remember being unimpressed at the time — but then, I didn't know what he was up to. His new citizenship made it possible for him to obtain residency in any of the countries of the European Union. He chose Holland.

I didn't know it, but at the time there was a tax treaty between Canada and the Netherlands that allowed Dutch residents to withdraw their Canadian RRSPs with no tax payable in either Canada or the Netherlands. That treaty is now under renegotiation. However, there are countries, such as Ireland, where you can withdraw your RRSP by paying a one-time shot of 15 percent to Canada. Not bad. If the funds are taken out in a country not having a tax treaty with Canada, the money is subject to a 25-percent-Canadian withholding tax, plus whatever the country of residence decides to claim. So, instead of withdrawing the money in Canada and paying the top marginal federal and provincial tax rates — roughly equivalent to 48 percent — Angelo became a resident of somewhere else and withdrew his RRSP at rock-bottom rates.

As well, having paid the tax and obtained the money, he is not required to pay Canadian taxes on the investment income. As far as Angelo is concerned, the money he uses is that which he earned in the past, and it has already been taxed to death.

I found out later, at a party Angelo threw for the local "cruisers," that there was a whole cadre of people sailing around the world who technically have their residencies in tax-benign locations, such as Ireland, and hence attract little or no tax liabilities.

If Angelo had stayed in Canada, he would have retired, rolled over his RRSP into an annuity, and paid taxes on the income as he withdrew it. Instead, he now has all the capital and pays no further taxes.

Obviously, the important part of this operation is the second citizenship, which allowed Angelo to obtain residency in a European country. I decided to look into my British background and my wife's Greek forefathers.* I could already see cracks in my rock of Sisyphus.†

"Angelo, give me the details. How did you do it?"

"I got my Italian citizenship and then obtained a copy of Revenue Canada's Information Circular 76-12R5. It is important to be precise when asking for the various pieces of information, as there is a great difference between information circulars, interpretation bulletins, and guides. The information circular listed all the countries that had treaties with Canada whereby foreign residents could obtain their Canadian RRSP funds tax free, or at reduced rates. That is important: a foreign 'resident' extracting his or her funds from Canada.

"Again, precision is paramount. In reading these bulletins, I noted exactly what kind of pension fund payment is subject to the favourable tax treatment. Does it refer to lump sums?

"Once I had settled on a country of residence — Hol-

---

* It should be noted that many countries such as Ireland do not require citizenship as a prerequisite to obtaining residency. For example, the Turks and Caicos Islands will grant residency upon the payment of $600 annually.

† Sisyphus was cursed by the gods to roll a rock up a hill for eternity. Every time he got it to the top, the rock rolled back down.

land — I wrote to Revenue Canada's International Taxation Office in Ottawa, and questioned them as to the accuracy of my interpretation of what taxes would apply to a one-time, lump-sum withdrawal of RRSP* funds by a resident of Holland. They have to tell you whether you are correct or not.

"I was now at the stage that I had a destination and knew what my tax status would be once I arrived there. However, the process wasn't over yet. You see, there is a great difference between residency and citizenship. Citizenship is an asset that allows you to be protected by a government. Therefore, citizenship is difficult to obtain. Residency is a liability that allows the government to exploit you, and is therefore bestowed on the unwary and difficult-to-dispose-of. Did you know, Stew, that in the U.K., touring foreign performers are deemed resident during their stay so that tax can be withheld from their British earnings? There is, of course, no question of bestowing citizenship on them, no matter how much tax is extracted.

"I now had to doff my Canadian residency and become a non-resident of Canada; in other words, a foreigner. Because residency is a liability to the individual but an asset to any government that can claim the resident, getting rid of residency is as difficult as getting rid of athlete's foot.

"In some cases, though, governments are more reluctant to classify individuals as residents. While the federal government desperately wants to classify you as a resident, most provinces don't want you to claim residency. You

---

* It is important to note that an RRSP is not a pension plan but a Registered Retirement Savings Plan. To be subject to the rules, the RRSP should first be rolled into an RRIF, which is the tax department's eyes is a pension plan. This is not onerous and guarantees compliance.

could fall into the unenviable position of being a resident of Canada, but not a resident of any province. Again, the reasons boil down to the liability-versus-asset consideration. If you are a resident of Canada, you are entirely a source of good, hard cash to the federal government. If you are a resident of a province, you will consume all sorts of services, from schooling for your children to heart transplants. Therefore, the federal government wants you, but the provinces don't.

"An acquaintance of mine kept an apartment in Toronto, although he spent 183 days a year in Florida. The feds deemed him a resident of Canada. He therefore decided to re-establish himself in Toronto, but was denied Ontario Health Insurance coverage because of his extended stay outside the province. Before the province would provide him with Ontario Health Insurance, he had to wait three months and pledge to stay in the province 364 consecutive days. In effect, the province wanted to make him a prisoner for one year. To make things worse, he had to pay the provincial portion of his taxes and was given no refund of his provincial sales tax, which full-fledged aliens receive. The only break he got was that he could claim his private health insurance premiums as a deduction (after reducing the amount by 3 percent of his income) from his taxable income.

"However, like everything pertaining to the government, form is as important as substance. Appearances count. There are steps you have to take. This is very similar to doing the tango. The steps must be followed religiously. Don't fret; it is not as hard as it sounds.

"The general rule is that you must permanently sever, or appear to sever, all ties with Canada. You can change your mind and return at some later date, but I wouldn't attempt it before two years had lapsed. Even then, you should be prepared to argue strenuously as to the changed circumstances that occasioned your return."

"Well, that's easy for you because you had somewhere to go. What about those who don't have somewhere to go?" I asked.

"How can you say that?" he asked. "There are many places in the world that would welcome you as a resident on a limited-time basis, even if you are not a citizen of the country. All you need is a visa and proof that you can support yourself. Many countries have consulates in Toronto and can set that up for you. You must be a non-resident of Canada during the period you are extracting your RRSP. Take a moment to review Information Circular 76-12R5, which I told you about earlier, and determine which country would have the lowest tax rate applicable to pension income. Once you have done this, phone or write to the country's consulate with the intent of obtaining a one-year resident visa. Places like Ireland would be more than happy to have you, as long as you don't undertake gainful employment, can show funds sufficient for the period of your stay, and have private health insurance."

"I see. I am just going to be a resident of some convenient place. But then I have to give up work, rent an apartment, and pay the cost of travel. Is it really worth it?"

"Stew, it is critical that you get your pension money out of Canada. Even if you have to pay the maximum withholding tax of 25 percent, you would be better off than leaving your money in Canada and continuously paying income tax on its earnings. Therefore, you have to find somewhere to go where you won't have to pay taxes on pension income. As I said, there are many countries that would love to have you as a resident. Your chore is to find the one that will accept you and best treats your RRSP as it leaves Canada and arrives at your destination. I found Holland. Read the Government of Canada's tax bulletins; they will assist you in determining where to go. Then find out if you can go there, either as a result of your wife's ancestors or your own. You may not even need to rely on ancestry."

"Angelo, why is it so important to get my pension money out of Canada?"

"Let's assume that you have a capitalized value of $500,000 in your pension. If you remove it from Canada properly, as a non-resident, you will pay a maximum of 25 percent, or $125,000. This will leave you with $375,000 to invest in a non-taxable annuity, providing you with income for 30 years of $39,780 per year, assuming a 10-percent compounded interest rate. If you left the money in Canada, you would have $500,000 to invest in your 30-year annuity at a 10-percent compounded interest rate, which would give you $53,040 per year before tax.

"At first glance, it appears you are $13,260 poorer (i.e., $53,040–$39,780) as a result of moving the money offshore. However, remember that you took the money out of Canada and bought an annuity in a tax haven. You have established residency in some lovely place that does not have taxation on foreign earnings. Therefore, your $39,780 is net to you, free of tax.

"The other alternative — to leave the money in Canada — leads to a tax liability of at least 40 percent on your $53,040, which would be $21,220, leaving you with an after-tax income of $31,820 (i.e., $53,040–$21,220). By keeping your pension in Canada, you are actually $7,960 worse off every year, which amounts to $238,800 paid to the government over the 30-year life of the annuity contract. As such, maintaining Canadian residency is costly, and you have to weigh the benefits. Let me write it out on paper for you. You'll then have the answers in black and white.

"That $7,960 savings more than covers the additional health and other costs you would incur by living outside Canada.

"As I mentioned before, Stew, it's possible to find countries residence where the withholding tax, because of tax

	Pension Domiciled in Canada	Pension Removed 25% Withholding	Pension Removed 15% Withholding
Principal Annuity	$500,000	$375,000	$425,000
Income (compoundedat 10%)	$53,040	$39,780	$45,080
Income Tax calculated at 40%)	$21,220	$0	$0
NET TO YOU	$31,820	$39,780	$45,080

treaties, is only 15 percent, in which case the net income to you will be even greater. And remember, Stew, I did this little example with a 40-percent tax rate. Move up to the more likely 50-percent rate and things look even more appealing. As well, you can choose a country of residence where the cost of living is lower. Imagine how much further your money would go in Spain, Italy, Portugal, Greece, or even the U.S.

"As you can see, if your total RRSP funds (yours and your spouse's) exceed $500,000, it makes great sense to take them out in total from abroad, even at the maximum withholding rate of 25 percent, if you don't have to pay tax in the country where you take up residence. As long as the withholding rate is less than the income tax rate, it makes sense to withdraw your RRSP funds. In the simplest terms, the difference between the withholding rate and the total provincial and federal income tax rate accrues to you.

"To some extent, you can receive the offshore benefit by leaving your pension funds in Canada, Stew, and simply paying the withholding tax as the money leaves Canada. The weakness in this approach is that you are assuming that the current withholding rate and your ability to take your pension money out of Canada will continue in perpetuity. I think it is wiser to pay the existing rate today because, if anything, the Canadian government will grow more avaricious with time, and either increase withholding tax rates or entirely restrict an individual's right to move capital out of the country.

"Don't look so surprised, Stew. Many countries, such as India, Hungary, and even the U.S., currently restrict the removal of money from their country."

"Angelo, you are mistaken. I heard that just recently the Bronfman family of Montreal took $3 billion out of the country without having to pay any tax."

"You are partially right. Revenue Canada turned down their scheme to remove the money tax free on three occasions. However, after seemingly divine intervention,* the tax department changed its mind and allowed the assets to

---

* Actually the intervention of a Senator owing his appointment to the Bronfmans.

leave without the payment of the $700 million in taxes due. That decision is being fought by an irate taxpayer named Harris and is still in the courts. So don't believe that without a friend in government you will be allowed to do the same thing."

"If I understand you, Angelo, you are advising me to take my money abroad because, if I retire and retain residency in Canada, I am going to have less money than if I live somewhere else."

"Correct, Stew," he said. "Let me put it in a different context. Suppose the bank that employs you offered you a job in Kamloops, B.C., or Calgary, Alberta, and told you that if you moved to the new location, they would pay you an additional $16,000 per year. This would result in $8,000 after tax in your pocket. You would then have more money, and at the same time a lower cost of living. Would you accept? I think so."

"But you make it sound so difficult to become a non-resident."

"No, it's not so much difficult as tedious."

"You said I had to sever all ties with Canada. What does that entail?"

"Well, let's start with the house, Stew. You are perceived for tax purposes to live or reside where you own a home."

CHAPTER 3

Is This Your House
OR IS THIS YOUR HOME?

"I chose to sell the house as I wanted the deal to be as clean as possible. You can, in fact, lease it out; however, you have to be careful to lease it in such a way that Revenue Canada won't be able to successfully argue that you have kept a dwelling place available for yourself in Canada. To give you an example, a guy I knew leased his house to his nephew on a month-to-month lease, and Revenue Canada deemed him to still be a Canadian resident. In other words, Revenue Canada does not want you to have even a toe in Canadian waters. Revenue Canada's general rule is that a Canadian resident who is absent from Canada for less than two years will be presumed to have retained Canadian resident status unless he or she can show that all Canadian ties were severed.

"There is another problem with leasing out the house, besides the ghastly position you are put into as a landlord. You will have a Canadian income stream as a result of the rental income. Yes, the house is now throwing money out to you. The folks at Revenue Canada don't like to see a buck go by that they don't have a piece of. So they will cut themselves in for 25 percent of any free cash generated by the house and paid to you as a non-resident."

"What do you mean by 'free cash,' Ang?"

"That's the profit from the vital income: the gross revenue less expenses."

"Hey, that's nasty," I said. "How can they justify charging you taxes when you don't consume any of the country's services?"

"You Canadians are really full of that fair-play nonsense, aren't you? If I told you I was going to give the rich more access to services than the poor, you would scream discrimination against the poor. If I prescribe tax rates higher for the rich than the poor, you accept this form of discrimination, which flies in the face of the spirit of the Canadian Charter of Rights. The tax system was never meant to be fair. It was meant to be politically beneficial. I remember how former finance minister Edgar Benson wanted to streamline the tax system and make it more equitable. It came out that if everyone paid 18 percent of their gross income to Ottawa, it would raise as much as the then-existing tax system, with its top rate of 48 percent. The difference would have been that multi-millionaires would have had to pay their fair share of taxes, or at least some taxes, and we couldn't have that."

"Well, I still don't think it's fair," I said.

"If you don't like withholding tax, don't pay it."

"What if they find out?"

"Stew, you are not thinking like a game player. Your kids would know how to handle this problem when playing *Dungeons and Dragons*! When you read the regulations, you will find that any free cash that is transferred abroad is subject to Canadian tax. The point is not to have any free cash in the house. So make the situation nice and clean and simple.

"Let's say your house is completely paid for and you rent it out for $2,000 per month, or $24,000 per year. Assuming expenses of $500 per month, this leaves free cash of $1,500 per month, or $18,000 per year. Taking into account the 25- percent withholding tax, you could expect $1,125 per month to reach you after tax ($1,500 - 25%). That works out to $13,500 cash to you per year.

"Let's look at another approach. If you mortgaged the house for $180,000 at 10 percent, the house would have an interest expense of roughly $18,000 per year, or $1,500 per month. This interest expense would effectively consume the free cash flow. You would have $180,000 in your hands from the mortgagee. Invest the $180,000 in provincial government bonds or good-grade corporate bonds issued for longer than 5 years and yielding 10 percent, and you would receive the equivalent of $1,500 per month, or $18,000 per year, without paying withholding tax."

"Yes, but is that legitimate?" I asked. "What about that law that says if you undertake something strictly for the tax benefits, then the action is nullified in the eyes of the tax department?"

"Well, there are two things to consider. First, you would

not be a taxpayer in Canada. Second, the tax department might find themselves on thin ice when trying to bring that rule into the withholding tax domain. Remember what Lord Curzon said in 1938?"

"I know you'll find this shocking," I said, "but I don't."

"In the case of *Westminster v. Inland Revenue*, which was tried in the highest court in England, the House of Lords, Lord Curzon ruled that 'a man had the right to arrange his financial matters in such a manner so as to incur the minimum amount of tax.'

"That judgment applies in Canada, as the country was under British rule at the time and the House of Lords was also the last court of appeal in Canada. So you are allowed to arrange your affairs in a similar manner. But you may not want to open a can of worms with the tax cowboys. I was told last month how the British tax escapists handle that problem. They either sell their houses to relatives with an option to buy them back at the same price, or sell them to domestic or offshore companies (which they own indirectly), depending on their personal circumstances. You would be amazed at how many companies in Jersey own houses in England. During the transaction, the house acquires a large mortgage."

"Wait a minute," I said. "Doesn't the foreign corporation have to pay taxes on the income or the capital gain?"

"In the first instance, Stew, the amount of the mortgage leaves no taxable income, and in the second instance, don't bet on a capital gain. If you are worried about the capital gain, then price the house at the high end of the market range. The other thing to keep in mind is that a number of these foreign countries do not have any income taxes."

"Let's put it on paper," I said.

"Okay, this is how the two scenarios look."

"Wait," I asked, "where does the $18,000 'cash received' in the second case come from?"

"That's the interest from the bonds. Remember, the mortgage proceeds of $180,000 were used to purchase the bonds, so you have to allow for the interest received on the bonds."

	Without Mortgage	With Mortgage
Annual Rental Income		
(12 x $2,000 per month)	$24,000	$24,000
Deduct		
Expenses ($500 per month)	($6,000)	($6,000)
Mortgage Expense	($180,000 at 10%)	($18,000)
Pre-tax Annual Rental Income	$18,000	$0
25% Withholding Tax	($4,500)	$0
Cash Received	$13,500	$18,000

"I like that," I said, "because I can't see any weaknesses."

"Pure and simple, it is financial engineering at its best: put the costs where they can do the most good, and the revenues where they receive the fewest penalties," Angelo said.

"That perverse smile of yours tells me there must be more."

"You know, as well, that you can transfer your house to your children or spouse almost cost-free in Ontario. Land-transfer tax in Ontario is based on the amount of the mortgage outstanding if the house is being transferred to a family member.

"Just last month, a bunch of us were sitting on the dock discussing the best way to handle a Canadian home when becoming a non-resident. A Canadian from Timmins, Mr. Jones, explained how he had transferred his $400,000 house to his son at fair market value. As part of the transfer, Mr. Jones took back a mortgage of $1,500. To avoid the argument by Revenue Canada that the house was not transferred at fair market value, Mr. Jones' son signed a promissory note agreeing to pay his father $398,500 ($400,000–$1,500). It was agreed that the promissory note would be free of interest, and that it would rank after the mortgage.

"I'm not sure I understand why the Joneses bothered with such a small first mortgage. Why didn't the son just make the promissory note for $400,000? It would have been so much easier," I said.

"The reason for the $1,500 mortgage was to ensure that the son could not sell the house or refinance it without notifying the mortgage holder. To make things easier, since Mr. Jones was no longer living in Canada, Mr. Jones decided to let his Canadian lawyer hold the mortgage."

"I get it, but wouldn't it have been easier, then, to have the mortgage in the amount of $400,000?" I asked.

"That wouldn't work. Remember, in order to reduce taxation, interest paid to the non-resident must be kept to a minimum. That's why any promissory note should be interest free. You can't personally place large mortgages with conventional interest rates against the property, as the interest collected would be subject to Canadian withholding taxes. You always have to keep in mind that Revenue Canada will do whatever it can to tax you."

"This sounds complicated, Ang," I said.

"It sounds complicated but, when you sit down and think about each step individually, it's not difficult.

Remember, your life and possessions are a complicated affair, and to unwind them takes as much or more care than putting them together. Also, there is an entity out there that doesn't want you to unravel the puzzle."

"Well, how did you handle it?"

"I wanted the best financial deal and as clean a break as possible, so I decided to sell the house."

"I can understand the 'clean break' part, but what about this 'best financial deal'?" I asked.

"Since I wouldn't be living in the house, I had to look at it as an investment asset and determine the return on investment. The options I had were to rent the house out and treat it as an investment, to mortgage the home and purchase bonds with the proceeds from the mortgage, or to sell it and make an alternative investment. So I did a financial analysis.

"I spoke with a few real-estate agents and I decided that I could probably sell the house for $350,000. If, on the other hand, I decided to rent, I figured my modest house would fetch about $1,600 per month on the market. These numbers are a little different from the ones we just looked at, so let's put the rental scenario on paper to get a clearer picture.

al Rental Income

2 x $1,600 per month)	$19,200
_ct	
Property Taxes	($2,400)
Insurance	($650)
Repairs	($500)
Pre-tax Annual Rental Income	**$15,650**
25% Withholding Tax	**($3,912)**
Cash Received	**$11,738**

"Now, as I mentioned, if I earned that $15,650 rental income per year, I would only receive 75 percent of it, having given up 25 percent in withholding tax to Revenue Canada. In other words, I would receive $11,738 on capital of $350,000 (the value of my house). That's a yield of 3.35 percent. That's nothing great when compared to bond yields of 10 percent.

"Therefore, let's apply the second option, my mortgaging and bond-reinvestment scenario. The beauty of this, if you remember, is that you can reduce the 25-percent withholding tax by offsetting the mortgage expense with the rental income."

Pre-tax Annual Rental Income	**$15,650**
Deduct	
Mortgage Expense	
(12 x $1,300 per month)	$15,600
Cash Received	**$50**

"Wait a minute," I said. "You lost me with that $15,600 mortgage expense."

"To end up with a $15,600 mortgage expense, I would

have had to take out about a $156,000 mortgage, assuming a 10-percent interest rate."

"Hey, I get it, that's smart."

"Now, with my $156,000 I would have reinvested in Hydro-Québec or other similar bonds yielding 10 percent, or $15,600 per year. When taken with the cash received of $50, or $37.50 after the notorious 25-percent withholding tax, I would end up with $15,637.50 on an asset worth $350,000. That's a yield of 4.5 percent. Still not great.

"My third option was to simply sell the house for $350,000 and invest the sale proceeds offshore in Government of Canada bonds yielding 10 percent. This would give me an income of $35,000 per year, free of any taxes. As you can see, I now have a yield of 10 percent, which is much better than 3.35 percent or 4.5 percent, wouldn't you agree?"

"All that sounds good on paper, Ang, but think of the capital gains you're missing out on if the house goes up in value," I said.

"What you have overlooked, Stew, is that if I were to make any capital gains on the house, whether in a corporation or through my personal hands, I would no longer have the luxury of the 'principal residence exemption' and I would have to pay Canadian income tax. That's because I would not be living in the house, but renting it out as a business. With this in mind, I would require significant appreciation to make it worthwhile for me to hang on to the house and collect the rental income."

"Eureka! I see it now, Ang. A house is a good investment only if you live in it."

"That's true, Stew, but only if you're a resident Canadian. You have the option to pay rent or a mortgage payment with your after-tax dollars. Included in all mortgage payments is a portion for repayment of principal; therefore, you are always increasing your capital worth or ownership in the house. Also, a house is a highly leveraged investment. You could own a $400,000 house with a down payment of $100,000 and a $300,000 mortgage. If the house increases in value by 10 percent you are $40,000 richer without an increase in your mortgage liabilities. Therefore, your gain would be $40,000 on an investment of $100,000 or 40 percent."

I hadn't thought of the leverage benefits to owner-occupiers in the residential real estate market, although I was well aware of the financial pitfalls from leverage in the speculative end of the residential market. I had seen the results on three occasions.

The first was at the bank where I worked. We had financed the building of a number of condominiums on the basis of contracts of sale for the units. How could you go wrong when the builder presented you with a sheaf of contracts showing that the building was 100-percent sold? Well, when the real estate market turned sour, it turned out that most of the buyers were speculators who had put up a small portion of the total cost of the units with the intention of selling them before completion. With no buyers in sight, the speculators were unwilling to follow through on their purchase contracts. They lost their deposits and we turned a short-term bridge loan into a long-term mortgage. The speculators were leveraging their small down payments against a potential increase in the condominium price. The lesson for the bank was that Toronto residential real estate was worth between $90 and $140 per square foot, and condominiums that were trading for $300 per square foot were out of touch with the real world.

My second exposure to residential speculation came when the fellow across the street from me sold his house at the top of the market with a conditional offer. This meant that the deal would not close if the purchaser could not dispose of some contingency, such as selling his house or obtaining financing. My neighbour should have been suspicious of the long closing required by the purchaser. However, when the market turned sour, the purchaser, who was obviously speculating, made sure that his conditions could not be met and therefore he did not end up with the house in a falling market. My neighbour lost the sale and wound up selling the house a year later for $50,000 less.

Even worse off was a cousin of mine who had a firm offer with a small down payment and a long closing. He bought another house on the strength of his sale, only to see his buyer take a walk and leave him with two houses. He had a tough time getting the deposit released as the real-estate company would not part with the money without the purchaser's approval. My cousin's lawyer told him that suing the purchaser would be costly, and even with a judgment there was little likelihood of collecting.

I concluded long ago that the real-estate market was structured by realtors for the benefit of the buyer at the vendor's expense. It was a great place to speculate as the real risks were minimal for the purchaser and enormous for the vendor. The purchaser could always walk away with only a small loss, in the form of a $10,000 deposit. At the same time, purchasers could potentially double their money before closing. After all, real estate, like pork bellies, is just a commodity.

I could see Angelo's thinking. For an investment market to be viable, it has to be liquid and equitable. The residential market is neither. Therefore, he was right not to count on his house as an investment.

I asked Angelo if the sale of the house was all that was needed for him to move offshore.

"That was only the first step," he said. "I still couldn't sit down — I was still dancing the 'Tango of Disentanglement.' Next came the financial connections. I could have no bank accounts, charge cards, or any other financial ties to Canada. I even moved my stock-brokerage account out of the country. If you decide to emigrate, remember that you will be deemed by Revenue Canada to have sold all of your property, including any securities. If the securities have gone up in value, you will have to pay capital gains tax on the securities' appreciation over their purchase price. So it is best to clean up your portfolio before departure.

"Of course, there can also be no binding ties with respect to employment, such as a contract that takes you back into employment in Canada after your return.

"To be dead sure that you are in fact dancing correctly, obtain Revenue Canada Interpretation Bulletin IT-221R2, 'Determination of an Individual's Residence Status.'* The bulletin covers all the details about furniture, cars, drivers' licences, and all that baggage of life. Also, be sure to note section 14, which states that if your departure is for tax purposes, other considerations might apply. It would seem imprudent to mention the tax benefits.

"You will then be confronted by the notorious NR73 form and its many queries. These are some of the questions you have to answer:

---

* See also Revenue Canada's "Living Outside Canada" and "Immigrants' and Emigrants' Tax Guide."

1. Are you married with a spouse who will stay behind in Canada?
2. Will you leave a child or grandchild in Canada who is dependent on you for support?
3. Will you continue to support a person who lives in a dwelling that you occupied before your departure?
4. Will you maintain a dwelling suitable for year-round occupancy by you or your family?
5. Will you own a rental residence with a lease that can be cancelled in less than three months?
6. Will you own a rental dwelling rented to a non-arm's length person?
7. Will you be storing your household effects in Canada?
8. Will you keep vehicles in Canada registered in Canada?
9. Will you keep your Canadian driver's licence?
10. Will you maintain provincial or territorial health coverage?
11. Will you maintain membership in Canadian social, recreational, or religious organizations?
12. Will you keep membership in professional organizations requiring Canadian residency?
13. Will you keep a bank account in Canada, or use Canadian credit cards?
14. Will you keep a seasonal residence in Canada?
15. Will you receive tax benefits or family allowance?

"It appeared to me that the questions were listed in order of importance; however, to be perfectly safe, I structured my departure so as to be able to answer no to all of them. Some people I have spoken to chose not to file an

NR73 as they felt it would just form a starting point for Revenue Canada to challenge their non-residency should they ever choose to return. The status determined by the questions is not binding, in any case. I know of circumstances where Revenue Canada had deemed a person resident of Ireland, and then decided it didn't like the results, so deemed him instead a resident of nowhere. This designation is particularly dangerous, because Revcan requires that, in order to be a non-resident of Canada, an individual be tax-liable somewhere else. So, if you're resident nowhere, Revenue Canada can take you back into the fold. If you are taxable and resident somewhere else and then give up that residency and acquire no other residency, you are still resident in the last place you resided. In the case of the Irish resident, he gave up his status after a year and went to sea. Revcan was angry with him, so they denied his Irish residency, even though he showed a chap at Revcan his Irish residency card, demonstrated he had rented an apartment for a year, and all the rest. They did not want him to be able to claim Irish residency while he was itinerant, so the Assistant Deputy Minister for International Taxation of the tax department cancelled his Irish residency with the stroke of a pen. So, you might ask, what good is an NR73?"

"Gosh, that sounds unfair — and probably illegal on the part of the tax guys,*" I said.

"Stewart, stop this instant! You can never mention taxation and the words 'moral,' 'fair,' or 'legal' in the same breath. Tax collection is all about money, and people's morality tends to become flexible when money is intro-

---

* For more on the criminal pursuits of CRA read *Tackling the Taxman*.

duced. The government needs your money, and it is there-fore unwilling to have your rights respected under the Charter of Rights and Freedoms or the Constitution. Thankfully, there is a growing volume of jurisprudence lim-iting the government's more blatant acts of immorality, but there is a long way to go. What the country desperately needs is someone to uphold the tax act."

"I thought that was the job of Revcan," I said.

"No, the *Income Tax Act* is a tool used by the tax collec-tors. It is a piece of legislation that they honour more in the breach than in the observance. Let me give you an example. There is a clause in section 231 of the act that prohibits the use of audits as a form of coercion and intimidation. I know of a person who was being hounded for a phony tax claim. When they found that he wouldn't pay and they couldn't collect from him, they harassed the lawyer for his wife's company and audited the company as well. I know it was harassment because the company had gross income of less than $65,000 annually, and when the audit was over it turned out Revcan owed the company money."

"I don't get it. Why was it a phony audit?"

"Stew, get a grip. How much more tax can you expect to get out of a taxpayer making $60,000 a year? Imagine if they had chosen at random a dentist earning $300,000 a year."

"She should have complained," I said.

"That's just it: to whom could she complain? There are no penalties outlined in the tax act for collectors or auditors who disobey the tax act. Only the taxpayers face penalties. If she had gone to the courts, as many brave Canadians have done, she might have won her case, the guilty would still have been left unpunished, and the results of the case would have been buried in the court records — if she could have found a court willing to hear the case."

"You can always appeal to the courts to right an injustice."

"Really? What about the Stephan case? In that instance, the federal tax collectors hounded Deborah Stephan so ruthlessly over a lousy $27,000 that she killed herself. So far, I have yet to see a conviction for her death against the two men involved, even though the circumstances of her death make it painfully clear that she killed herself because of them.

"When you file a tax form, you are setting up a de facto contract with the tax collectors. Though taxpayers are never informed of this contract, it has led, in some cases, to their suicides. Under the circumstances, I would say that giving pieces of paper to Revcan is dangerous to your health — hence the reluctance to file an NR73. However, sometimes you have few alternatives. If you want to have your status determined immediately to facilitate the removal of your RRSP from Canada and to sever your ties, then you have to file the form. Your alternative is to stay out of the country for two years, at which point you will be deemed a non-resident of Canada if you can show you are tax-liable in another country. Listen to the words carefully, Stew: they say you have to be liable to pay. That does not mean you have to have paid."

"So those are your two choices: either file an NR73 or stay away for two years?"

"Not quite. You could go to the Turks and Caicos Islands and pay $600 to establish residency there. If you have an address and residency granted by the government of a country, it is difficult even for the fertile minds at

Revcan to find you in two places at one time. It would defy the laws of physics, not those of Canada."

"Why did you file one, Ang?"

"I wanted to resolve my residency status as soon as possible, rather than having to wait two years before I could get my RRSP and get on with my life. As well, I feared that, in two years, changing circumstances might preclude my getting my money or status.

"Before departing, I wrote to Holland and confirmed that no tax would be payable in Holland on funds received from my RRSP. I then moved to Holland, rented a flat, and did all the things required by IT-221R2. With my flat lease signed and all my criteria met, I then wrote to Revenue Canada and asked them to ascertain my residence for tax purposes. They had to do this to know what rate of tax applied to me. Once they had deemed me to be a resident of Holland, and therefore a non-resident of Canada, I sent a copy of the letter and IC-76-12R4 to the trust company holding my RRSP and asked them for the funds.

"By law, if there is withholding tax due on funds and the payer does not deduct these taxes, then the payer is responsible for the amount. The trust companies are, as you would expect, very careful to be sure that everything is in order before they disburse any funds. Therefore, to make it easy for them, I had everything documented.

"Also, remember that you are going to have to pay income tax on the income received during your last year of residence in Canada. To maximize the benefits of my new status, I departed the country on December 31 so that I could claim a province of residence at year end. Otherwise I would have lost some deductions and paid a higher rate on my last year's income.

"So there I was, starting the year 1990 in a new country with all my RRSP funds and no tax liability. My residence was in Holland, my home in Spain, and my heart in Italy."

"How could you become a resident of Holland?" I asked.

"It was easy because I held a European Union (EU) passport as a result of my Italian passport. This allowed me to live anywhere in the EU. However, most countries will allow you to take up temporary residence if you can show that you are not going to be a financial drain. Usually, these residencies are granted on the basis of a year's right to reside, as opposed to an immigrant visa. However, if you really want to have flexibility, get an EU passport if possible."

Angelo was moving through this faster than I could imagine him doing anything. This was not the guy I knew in Toronto, who would take ten minutes to come to a three-no-trump bid. I had to pause and collect my thoughts. What had he done?

1. Using the dictates of Revenue Canada, he had made himself a non-resident of Canada.
2. Using the criteria of Revenue Canada, he had made himself a resident of a country that had a tax treaty with Canada, ensuring that his pension plan funds could be withdrawn from Canada and received in his new country of residence in the most tax-effective manner.
3. Having obtained from Revenue Canada recognition of his new residential status, he had withdrawn all his pension funds free of tax.

The other difficulty I was having in accepting all of this

was the sale of the old homestead. The sale of a home is a real commitment. It is, in effect, saying, I am not coming back. There are two sides to the sale. The good side is that you are making a commitment. Plus, the financial consid-erations all point to a sale as the best course of action.

The bad side is that selling a home entails a terrible toll emotionally. Not the house — the home. Selling is prob-ably the best course of action when you are in the departing mode. On the other hand, though, it can all seem so brutal. I asked myself, What if I wanted to return? I would be out of the real-estate boom in Toronto. But then, as Angelo pointed out, the only thing that makes a real-estate boom is the tax-free aspect of the capital gains on the house because of the "principal residence exemp-tion." If my funds were in a tax-free environment offshore, I could probably outperform the housing market in any case. Anyway, it's dangerous to get into that mindset about real estate. I remember when, on a square-foot basis, condos were selling for more than mansions. A year later, condos were selling with the same frequency that people were winning the lottery. In fact, I think that in Toronto, in some months, there were more lottery winners than condo buyers. Most of my friends who were stampeded into buying condos in the late 1980s had negative net worth in their abodes in the 1990s. So Angelo was right. The intelligent investor recognizes that there is no sure thing and keeps investments separate from emotions.

I was also disturbed by the thought of what my wife's attitude would be to a plan like Angelo's. I figured the best way to get the inside story was to go to someone who had done it. I looked for Angelo's wife, Sarah.

She had just finished hanging her laundry on the lifelines and was preparing to go into town to shop. I asked if I could tag along and help. She said she'd be happy for the company.

"Sarah, how have you weathered this enormous change in your life?" I asked.

"It is not such a great change, Stew. You probably remember that Ang and I were taking longer and longer vacations, until he was taking a full month in the summer. In that way, the idea of our being away sort of grew on me."

Yeah, I thought. "So what you're saying is, you see this just as an extended holiday?"

"I did originally, but now it has become a way of life," she said.

"Well, weren't you afraid to leave?"

"No. I realized it had to be done. Angelo showed me his pay stubs from the 1970s and the current ones. Add to those the direct taxes, like the provincial and federal sales taxes, and I could see that he was working longer for less. I didn't see that as fair to him.

"He then went on to explain how much money we would have and promised we could go anywhere, live anywhere I wanted to, after he finished his trip to the Mediterranean. To be honest, at this point, I hope it never ends. I have had some time to experience the constraints of our new lifestyle and I don't see any problems. Angelo went over the finances carefully with me in the first instance, so I had no real strong fears, only a fear of the unknown.

"I miss my friends. But I hope to see many of them during the summer. Our boat and its location are quite a draw. Look at you. How long did you have to deliberate about coming over to see Ang?"

She was right. I had jumped at the chance. I couldn't

see anyone in his or her right mind not taking up the offer. And I was noticing more and more of my friends, who were a few years older than I, leaving for exotic retirements. So far, I had received invitations to Spain, Greece, and Mexico.

"When you left, did you know that you would be living on a boat?"

"Angelo and I had discussed our future at great lengths. We considered buying a recreational vehicle and touring Europe, but then discovered that RVs offer too great a temptation to European thieves. We looked as well at a canal boat and a tour of Europe by the canal system. We concluded we would do that, but only when we were too old to sail. Once we had made up our minds to sail, we took sailing lessons and chartered boats in the Caribbean."

"What are your regrets about the departure and this gypsy way of life?" I asked.

"As I mentioned, I do miss my friends. That said, other women with similar lifestyles have told me to take the $1,200 cure and get over it."

"What's the $1,200 cure?"

"It's the $1,200 you pay for a plane ticket to go home for a month to visit your 30 nearest and dearest friends, only to discover how quickly they have forgotten you and your existence. Many of the women I have spoken to have taken the cure, finding it almost indispensable and certainly very therapeutic. I guess I am going to have to go through it."

"Don't you worry about your financial situation?"

"I did at first. I was overly frugal and tried to stop Ang from eating at restaurants all the time and spending a lot of money on the boat. I noticed after a couple of months that

I always had money left over from my budget. I hadn't calculated that we had almost doubled our income by leaving. Then I realized my spending was way down on hairdressers, cleaning ladies, health clubs, and the like. So on the expenditure side, I started to feel that I didn't have a problem. Ang pointed out that with our conservative bond investments, we would always have a revenue stream. In his business, on the other hand, we never knew how long the good or bad times would last, nor did we know Ang's job would always be there. I concluded that our new income set-up was by far more secure than what we had in the past."

"But doesn't this gypsy lifestyle make you feel insecure?"

"No. For once in my life, I know that what we own is ours. No imposition of wealth or estate tax, or any other devious government behaviour, can take away from us what we own."

"I gather that you were pretty well convinced of the viability of your new lifestyle by the time you left," I said.

"Yes, at an intellectual level I was convinced that we would be fine, but I still had visceral doubts and these, Ang explained, could only be overcome by experience. You can't explain high diving to someone in a way that will allay all their fears. They have to jump."

I could see that Angelo had sold her the way he used to sell his partners on a new deal. Before his presentation, he sat down with the numbers and proved his financial thesis. He then thought of all the possible questions and concerns and researched the answers. He obviously had done a great selling job on Sarah, but then, if he hadn't, he wouldn't be here. This was probably the most important selling job of his life.

I was still nagged by the return question. What if? Had Angelo in his cool accountant's manner thought that one out? The answer would have to wait. I still couldn't see the big picture. I didn't know where his wealth had come from and where it was now. As I walked back with Sarah, I wondered where he had stashed his money. After carrying the groceries below, I went on deck and hit Ang with the big question.

"Angelo, that's great. I know where your residence, home, and heart are, but where is the money?"

CHAPTER 4

Penny, Penny,
WHO'S GOT THE PENNY?

....

"Well, Stew, that's an interesting question and it depends on who's asking. My old Italian grandmother used to tell me to never show or flaunt wealth, as that created envy and avarice on the part of those who observed it.* Tax collectors are the world's most avaricious observers.

"What I had to do was make my money invisible. This involved creating a company, moving the funds into that company, and then moving them partially out. Let me explain.

---

* This is very pertinent advice. In Toronto and other Canadian cities facing the growing incidence of home invasions, one of the best lines of defence is to not have an ostentatious lifestyle.

"At my stage in life, I only want to own interest-paying bonds or debentures. However, in case of problems with some rapacious tax collector, I don't want to have securities in my name. You never know when someone will walk down a wharf somewhere, tell you that you've just been declared a resident, and demand a portion of your income in the name of income taxes. What I have done is registered the securities in the name of Zeus Corp., which I established in the Turks and Caicos Islands, a well-known Caribbean tax haven. The corporation cost me $2,000 to set up. I don't own any shares in Zeus Corp., but when I am interested in purchasing bonds or debentures the company does my bidding. When I obtained my RRSP funds, I lent them to Zeus at no interest. Zeus then bought government bonds and had them registered in the name of the company, which has an address in the Turks and Caicos Islands. If anyone checks the records for those bonds, they will see that the bonds are owned by a corporation in the Turks and Caicos Islands, and that the corporation is the recipient of the interest. I physically possess the bonds but I don't own them."

"That seems like a lot of effort," I said. "What does it gain you?"

"Wait a minute, Stew. Let's look at those two questions one at a time. You implied it was a lot of effort. There used to be an easier way, which was to buy bearer bonds. As you know, these were not registered either as to principal or interest, and were issued with coupons attached for interest. When interest was due, you merely took the coupon to the bank and demanded cash. In years gone by, most bonds were issued in bearer form. These bonds, which offered the possibility of tax deferral, have slowly disappeared from the scene as governments have grown more rapacious. United States tax authorities now demand that all bonds be registered in the name of the final interest recipient or have the interest due deducted at source. I expect that this model will be followed by most governments."

"With the demise of bearer bonds, what can you do now?"

"I've thrown in the towel and gone to the registered bond format. I have the corporation buy the bonds, either through a bank or stockbroker, and register them in the company name. The interest payments go to the address given during the registration process. Originally, when I was very paranoid, I had the bonds delivered to me in registered form and the interest payments sent to the address of my mail forwarder. In that way, I actually possessed the asset in my hands and was in control of the flow of interest funds. The funds, once deposited in the corporate bank account, could be accessed by us either through cheques drawn on the account or by debit card. At my second level of paranoia, I had all the transactions done through the bank and left the bonds with the bank, but took out insurance covering loss of the funds with an English insurance company. The cost of this insurance was only 20 basis points,* which meant I was paying $2,000 per million dollars for insurance. The low rate for the premium told me that the loss rate must be minimal, so I eventually let the insurance drop."

---

* A basis point is 1/100 of 1 percent, so 20 basis points is 20 percent.

"You've gone to a lot of trouble and expense. Is it worth it?"

"Well, if I am sued, there is nothing to take hold of except a few bucks in the bank. If the tax collectors of some jurisdiction want to rip me off, there is nothing for them to attach. I don't even own this boat. It also alleviates my estate problems.

"Being one of those 'green eye shade' conservative accountants, as you and the guys used to call me, I set up my situation to be bulletproof. Let's look at it:

1. My assets are not in my name.
2. My assets are owned by a corporation that is opaque to prying eyes.
3. The corporation is located in a jurisdiction with complete bank and corporate secrecy.

"It is now impossible for anyone to determine what I own, never mind take it away from me. Remember when my house was broken into and the police came by? What did they advise? Equip the home with deterrent devices, such as bars on basement windows, locked gates, double-keyed access doors, and lots of lighting. When I asked if that would ensure that my home wouldn't be broken into, the police explained that the deterrents merely make it more difficult for the burglar. The criminal would assess the deterrents and then conclude that it was easier to break into somebody else's house. The same applies to tax collectors. None of them want to tackle myriad protection devices. If they perceive the task is too difficult, they will move on to another target.

"That is particularly important over here. I read just

this morning of a radio-and-TV-station owner in Greece who criticized the government and incurred its wrath. The government couldn't find any shortcomings in his licences, so it proceeded to tackle him on the basis of his income tax."

"Come on, Angelo, you said yourself that this was more likely to occur over here, not in North America. It couldn't happen in North America."

"How did the U.S. government attack Al Capone? Through the tax system,"* he said. "Read the tax cases if you want some amusement on those long Canadian winter nights. The one that amused me the most was *Minister of National Revenue v. Mrs. MacDonald.*"

Angelo was, like most accountants, not prone to real thigh-slappers when it came to amusing stories. However, he was my host, so I encouraged him. "Tell me about it," I said, with dread.

"Mrs. MacDonald was a well-known madam in Vancouver. She ran an exclusive brothel that catered to the West Coast's upper crust. Needless to say, in spite of many complaints, there was little incentive on the part of the local officials, who were mostly clients, to take any action to close her operation.

"However, the local bluestocking crowd decided that something should be done about Mrs. MacDonald's house, so they went after her claiming that she was evading income taxes. They obviously thought that a woman who was, in their eyes, immoral would also be a tax evader.

---

* The tax system in Canada has been used to attack enemies of the Party such as Stephen Le Drew and Tim Issac. The system has been used to allieviate the tax burdens of the Party faithful such as Paul Martin and the Bronfman family.

They reported Mrs. MacDonald to the Department of National Revenue, as it was called in those days.

"Well, the old girl hadn't been around for all those years because of stupidity. She, like you and I, believed in paying her fair share of taxes. For 15 years, she had filed tax returns declaring the income from her brothel.

"As is human nature, the tax sleuths couldn't just give up on their investigation, having dedicated so much time and money to the enterprise. They seized on the fact that Mrs. MacDonald had included, as expense items in the operation of the brothel, the cost of numerous cases of liquor purchased at Christmas and distributed, according to Mrs. MacDonald, in varying amounts to local policemen and officials, depending on their offices.

"The tax department declared that these were gifts, given freely on the part of Mrs. MacDonald. She claimed they were bribes to ensure the continuance of her business, and hence a necessary expense.

"The judge — we don't know, of course, if he had first-hand knowledge of Mrs. MacDonald's enterprise — found that the madam was running an illegal business and, as such, would be required to ensure a level of oversight on the part of the police. The distribution of liquor at Christmas to the police would encourage oversight on their part and hence did, in fact, constitute a legitimate business expense.

"Mrs. MacDonald continued her illegal activity of living off the avails of prostitution, offering bribes, and maintaining a bawdy house. However, more important in the eyes of the government, she paid her taxes."

"Angelo, I can't believe that. What you're telling me is that the government felt justified, on the one hand, in out-

lawing bawdy houses, and yet was willing to tax the proceeds from this operation. The government was itself, in
effect, living off the avails of prostitution."

"As I said, Stew, the case is, or was, written up in the
CCH *Tax Reporter* as late as 1975. In Canada, the government is serious enough about taxes that, although it will
not allow the police to enter a domicile without a search
warrant in the case of murder, it does allow entry and
seizure without a warrant for tax purposes."

"I find that hard to believe," I said. "What about the
Charter of Rights and Freedoms?"

"Stew, let me put to rest the myth that the Charter of
Rights and Freedoms protects you from your government." Angelo went to his chart table and started
rummaging around. He then produced this clipping from
the January 22, 1999, edition of the *Globe and Mail.*

Top Court Backs Revenue Canada

The Supreme Court of Canada proved unwilling yes-
terday to strip Revenue Canada of its extraordinary
powers to delve into the financial affairs of Canadian
citizens.

In a swift and resounding victory for federal government lawyers, the court reinstated a special inquiry
into possible tax evasion by prominent Toronto devel-
oper Angelo Del Zotto.

The court announced its ruling within hours of
conclusion of an oral appeal of a 1997 decision by the
Federal Court of Appeal. In its earlier 2–1 ruling the
lower court had struck down the right of Revenue
Canada to set up special inquiries.

Inquiries can subpoena individuals and seize documents, despite the absence of any requirement to persuade an impartial judicial officer that there are reasonable and probable grounds behind the demands. Even police officers investigating criminal offences lack this power.

Nonetheless, the Supreme Court agreed with federal lawyers that the inquiries do not violate the right to avoid self incrimination or to be free of unreasonable search and seizure.

"I'm extremely pleased at the result and that it was so swift and clear," said the federal lawyer. "I think it is fair to say that had the decision gone the other way, a lot of doors would have been closed in regard to the enforcement of legislation involving income tax and other forms of tax," he said.

When it struck down the special inquiry provision the Federal Court of Appeal said that inquiries are more akin to criminal than to regulatory investigations. It said they violate the right to privacy by allowing investigators to pore freely over papers likely to contain intimate personal information.

In their response federal lawyers argued that, even if the investigative techniques did violate the Constitution, they were justifiable in a system of government that depends greatly on tax revenue. That argument was accepted by the Supreme Court of Canada.

My first thoughts — that Angelo was being paranoid with all this emphasis on "opaqueness" and "bulletproofing" — were now put to rest. I began to see that he had looked into this in some detail. I remember how, when I was having an extension put on my house, the work started to fall behind because my architect was becoming unavailable. I thought perhaps he had too much work, but when I called, his secretary told me that there was a man from the tax department who had taken up residence in their office and had been going over the books for two months. He demanded and received my architect's unstinting attention. In the end, the audit resulted in the recovery by Ottawa of a few thousand dollars with no criminal proceedings. However, my extension was delayed by a month and my architect told me that he believed the whole exercise cost him $10,000 in lost time and extra expenses. The irony of it was he suspected that the audit had been instigated by his former wife in a fit of vindictiveness. You never know who is waiting in ambush.

One of my neighbours, whose business allowed for potential cash sales, took out an insurance policy, so to speak, against future audits. He anonymously reported himself to Revenue Canada as a tax cheat in the guise of an unnamed, disgruntled former employee. He had been scrupulous in his tax reporting up to the time of the audit and was therefore given a clean bill of health. When he went through a messy divorce some years later, he was not subject to an audit, although he was sure his former spouse reported him to Revenue Canada. I've since heard of other occasions of anonymous self-disclosure to Revenue Canada. You might call it indecent exposure.

I could see Angelo's situation. He, like all of us, could never know when someone might walk up and threaten an audit or demand a tax payment. The threat to comply would be seizure of one's goods and chattels. Angelo didn't have any. Everything he possessed was owned by a company residing quietly on some sunny island.

"I see what you've done, Angelo. You've put a layer of insulation between you and anyone who may want your assets. That's sharp."

"That's not all," he said. "There are ancillary benefits. I don't believe it is prudent to give grown children large sums of money. However, faced with the prospect of dying and paying my assets out to my sons or to a government, it would seem to me there would be less harm caused on a global basis if my boys got the money. Anyway, I can't see why my demise should be considered a taxable undertaking, if you'll pardon the pun. Therefore, under the terms of my arrangement with the trust company holding the shares of Zeus, the shares will go to my sons at my death. This will be done without estate taxes or probate fees."

"Okay, so you don't own anything. How do you live? Where did the money for those cigars come from? Where did you get the money?"

"Stew, you haven't changed. You are still the investment banker who wants to know everything immediately. Settle down, you're in Spain. It's nine o'clock and you will soon be hungry."

"Hold it, Ang, hunger can wait. Let me see if I have it right. You've paid for the incorporation of an offshore company in a jurisdiction with corporate and bank secrecy, and it owns all your worldly goods."

"Right, Stew. The company, because it is classified as an 'exempt company' is under no obligation to disclose any information to any inquiring agency, not even who the directors are. The shares of the company are held by a trust company."

"Ang, I can't see how you have any control over the situation," I said. "How do you gain control or pass on control?"

"To tell you the truth, control really doesn't mean anything to me. As long as I have possession of all of the assets, I have no worries. This is a perfect example of the old saying, 'possession is nine-tenths of the law.'"

"But what if the trust company decides to sell the shares or even give them away? This is all of your life savings!"

"You never miss a trick, do you, Stew? I thought of that, too, and so I made sure that the trust company couldn't dispose of the shares. I had the trust company issue a warrant to me entitling my heirs to buy all the shares in Zeus that the trust company was holding for $10 upon my death. This accomplished two things. It stopped the trust company from disposing of the shares because there was an option outstanding in the form of the warrant they had issued. Plus, it allowed me to pass on the assets without some form of inheritance tax."

"I don't get it, Ang. How does that protect you?" I asked.

"Slow down, slow down, I'll tell you. It protects me in two ways. First, since I don't have the ability to exercise the warrant to gain control of the company, Revenue Canada can't deem me to be, in fact, in control of Zeus by arguing that I have an option to acquire all of the shares. Second, and more important, the trust company can't dispose of the shares because they never know when I might die. At any time, someone could show up with the warrant and $10 requesting all of the shares in Zeus."

"But can't Revenue Canada say that the heirs have control of Zeus through the warrant and then attribute the company's earnings to them?"

"No, Stew, because exercising the warrant requires my death, an event over which Sarah and my sons have no control, I hope!"

"Another well-thought-out plan, very impressive," I said. "You mentioned earlier that the company purchases the government bonds for you. How does that work?"

"Good question. Zeus opened a stock-brokerage account in a Turks and Caicos Islands brokerage firm. This company, in turn, opened an account at the brokerage of my choice somewhere in the U.S. or Canada. That last broker was required to issue a letter restricting where the assets in the account could go. Because of the structure of the company, they can go only to me or my heirs. When I want to buy or sell any shares, I call the Turks broker, who then places the order with the North American broker. Because of the restrictions imposed by the letter, the North American broker must keep the securities or pass them on to the particular member in the corporation. As it stands, all my securities are resting with a major bank brokerage in Canada. The brokers required certain forms to be signed and returned to authorize the opening of the account and my appointment as portfolio manager."

"That seems a little obtuse, Ang. Why didn't you just have the company, Zeus, open an account with a bank or North American broker? You realize, of course, that a bank can buy securities for an account holder, and many European banks still do that."

"In the old days, that was how these structures worked. A company was formed in a jurisdiction that had bank and corporate secrecy. That corporation would then open a bank and stock account with the most reputable bank it could find in the jurisdiction, quite often Barclays. The individual who formed the corporation would be appointed as the signing authority on the account. As you can see, it was all very clean and simple. However, in recent years, the U.S. and the EU have put pressure on the banks. To protect themselves, the banks have added a question to their account-opening forms that asks, 'Who is the *beneficial* owner of the company?' In other words, not the titular owner, but the person who, when all the smoke clears, will benefit from the activities of the corporation. The local brokers in the tax havens are under no such restrictions.

"This structure also gets around the problem of opening stock accounts in North America. Many years ago, the brokers were placed under the 'Know Your Client Rule' so that investments in the client account would always be appropriate to the client's wealth profile. The investment regulators didn't want to see high-flying dot-com companies showing up in the portfolios of 80-year-old widows. Those rather benign rules have now been turned on their heads, so that a broker must intimately know who the client is; that way, no nasty tax avoiders show up on the firm's books. There is no law or legislation at work here; it is just a courtesy to the tax department as a result of a little arm-twisting. However, there is a long-established practice of brokers acting for other brokers, from which comes the term 'jitney and two-dollar brokers.' Thus, a foreign broker opening a segregated account in a major house in North America goes unchallenged."

"Aren't you worried about the integrity of the broker in the Turks?" I asked.

"No, because none of the assets are in his hands except the interest cheques he receives from the investments, which he then passes on to my bank. If I was concerned, I would purchase insurance on the amounts in the Turks brokerage account."

"Ang, if I did this, wouldn't it be tax evasion?"

"No, Stew, this is tax avoidance. There is a very big difference. When you undertake to lie or defraud Revenue Canada, you are evading taxes, which is a crime. That's why your tax statement is like a sworn statement.* You have to reveal all your sources of income. You do not have to reveal the income sources of General Motors or any entity over which you have no control."

"I understand all that, but if I set up a company, the government will attribute all of its income to me," I said.

"Of course. That's because there is little difference between you and the company. In Revenue Canada's eyes, you are doing business under another name, but it is still you. Unless you can show that you do not have control of the company, the tax folks will say it is you and attribute the income to you. If you don't want to have the income attributed to you, don't own or control the company. All the ruses have been tried, such as setting up a company with non-voting shares convertible to voting shares, and the direction of the company being taken by a non-voting shareholder. It doesn't work. As soon as Revenue Canada sees who the final beneficiary is, they attribute the income to that person in the year it is earned."

"That may be so, but I know there are rich guys all over

---

* The signing of a tax form establishes a de facto contract between Revenue Canada and the individual, by which he or she becomes a taxpayer and is so described in the *Income Tax Act*. A number of organizations have grown in Canada disputing the use and foundation of such contracts. Although these challenges have some basis in law, the reality is that if these contracts and the collection of income tax are found to be ultra vires, the government will institute new measures without debate.

Canada evading taxes."

"Hold it, Stew: wrong word. You mean avoiding taxes, and they are doing so either with the government's blessing or to its dismay. Don't forget, Parliament allowed the setting up of trusts to allow the wealthy to pass on their assets without the benefit of taxation at death. This, like some of the other abuses that Ottawa condones, is under constant examination.

"The avoidance of tax that dismays Ottawa is the use of offshore corporations in tax havens. These systems work by divorcing the beneficiary of a corporation's efforts from ownership. The earnings don't fall within Canada's jurisdiction and cannot be attributed to a Canadian. The systems work through the use of corporate and bank secrecy and they are perfectly legal. The best schemes are the simplest and, as is the case with most things, the most expensive one is not necessarily the best.

"Therefore, when you talk about the reduction of people's tax bills, you have to be careful to distinguish between avoidance and evasion."

Angelo's dissertation was beginning to make sense, but I was starting to feel that there had been an avoidance of benefits for my body. My stomach was growling and I needed sustenance, not to mention a drink. I thought it time to make my needs known to Angelo.

"Wow, Ang, it's after nine. Is it too late to get dinner?"

"It's still early by Spanish standards. They don't start dinner here until nine."

We walked along a well-lit, narrow, winding street. The buildings were whitewashed, similar to the fashion in Greece, and the shops were just closing. I thought back to Toronto and realized it was three o'clock in the afternoon when I would ordinarily have been trying to keep my head off my desk after a "rock crusher" lunch spent trying to drum up some business or cement some deal. If things went well, I'd probably go over to see Harry at his men's shop and buy some outlandish rag, like a $2,000 suede jacket, the skin of which had been chewed into suppleness by the gums of nine-month-old Peruvian children, high in the Andes. On the other hand, if the deal fell out of bed, I'd get drunk at the bar at the top of our building and pray to God I didn't get picked up by the cops while stupidly driving to Oakville.

Ang led me to something that looked like a sushi bar. The difference was that the ceiling was hung with what appeared to be the hind legs of some beasts, and the little glass case along the bar contained only two things I could recognize: baby octopus and squid. The rest of the stuff consisted of stews, barbecues, and salads.

He ordered a bottle of wine and some *hamon*. The wine arrived in an unmarked bottle with the cork half out. "Loblaws' President's Choice?" I asked.

"Almost. This is a bodega. If you look at the rear wall, you will see the barrels of wine, which they buy from the local vintner. They pour the wine from the barrel into the bottle to sell it. Actually, speaking of that, let's have a bottle of their Cava."

Ang pushed the wine aside and asked for Cava seco when the barman arrived with the *hamon*, which I determined to be ham. The ham, it turned out, was being cut from the legs I saw hanging from the ceiling. What looked like a champagne bottle was put in front of us, this time unopened. The bartender removed the cork with a resounding report and poured the bubbly into the two champers flutes in front of us. I tried it. It was fabulous.

"Ang," I said, "hold on. I know you are on a fixed income. Don't blow the family budget in one night."

"Look, no offence, old buddy, but this only costs $5 a bottle."

"Ang, this is champagne, you must be kidding."

"Yes, it's like so many other things you see in life; often the label belies the content. Here they can't call it champagne because the grapes aren't grown in that region of France. So they call it Cava and it tastes like champagne. Over here, it's the water that's expensive."

As I sipped my Cava, I thought about what Ang had told me. Basically, there were reputable countries and banks out there somewhere that were helping people avoid taxes. They did this by establishing corporate and bank secrecy. It could be said that Ang was disobeying the spirit of the law, while abiding by the letter. But on what else are tax-avoidance schemes based? I started to wonder about the morality of his undertaking, and then thought about the printing firms that work on political campaigns only to reap the later reward of producing useless government advertising that describes how wonderful the government is. Then, of course, there are the citizenship judges and parole board appointments for failed candidates or cabinet ministers' girlfriends. Christ, I can remember when the boys in Ottawa gave some Toronto billionaires a $48-million tax break, in the name of nationalism, to take over an oil company that they went on to strip and enfeeble. You could say Angelo was, as his name implied, an angel compared to the pork-barrelling going on in Canada. Angelo was being right up-front and avoiding taxes. Very legal. So he wasn't following the spirit of the law. Who believes in spirits anyway?

It occurred to me that Ang had his fortune, whatever

that might be, in bonds in a brokerage house somewhere in North America, held in the name of a foreign corporation that received all his interest cheques. But the real question was, how did he live?

CHAPTER 5

Will That Be Visa
OR VISA?

....

I decided to slow my intake of goodies long enough to get Angelo going again.

"Ang," I said, "those guys in that company in the funny country get all your interest payments. How do you get the money to live?"

"Because I am a non-resident of Canada, I have signing authority on the corporate bank account and merely transfer the interest payments to my bank in one of the Channel Islands. From there, I either use my credit card or pay by cheque. When dealing with some of these English banks, you'll find quite a difference in attitude from the Canadian banks we're used to. These offshore banks are very service-oriented. They have to be because of the competition.

"I would have thought, Stew, that as an investment type, you would know that bond holders can provide any address they like for the payment of their interest. In this case, I use the corporate account that is in the same bank as my personal account. It is merely an in-bank transfer to move the funds. Some of the bonds are held in the name of the stockbroker and pay their interest to the corporation's stock account in the Turks and Caicos Islands. The brokerage company then immediately transfers that payment to my bank in the Islands."

"But what if that interest payment, for whatever reason, doesn't get paid to the bank in the Channel Islands, or the brokerage company decides to take a little extra for their trouble?"

"Gee, Stew, you are the untrusting type, aren't you? It's a good question, though. I am at risk for one interest payment. However, should the money not be transferred to my bank, I would immediately take over control of the bonds by the privileges accorded to me in my corporate structure or instruct the trustees holding the shares of the company to take whatever action was necessary. Remember that I said you could buy insurance to cover any amount of principal in the brokerage accounts."

"All this must be costly," I said.

"Let's say you are looking at $30,000 in interest payments semi-annually. You would lose about one day's interest and the transfer costs of $35. In total, that is about $200. If you had done that within a tax system, it would have cost about $15,000. Which do you think is more costly?"

I still wondered how Ang met his daily expenses. It's nice to have a big fat account in Jersey or Guernsey, but how do you get your hands on the money? I, as usual, went for the straightforward approach.

"Ang, how did you get the money to pay for tonight's dinner?"

"I have a VISA debit card issued by my bank. Because it is a debit card, I pay no interest on the withdrawals but only a minimal service charge. If I want, I can charge to the card. The only downside is that, it being a debit card, if anyone gets the PIN number and the card at the same time, they could clean out my account. Because of this, I keep only working levels in the debit account.

"If I need large amounts of cash, I phone my bank and ask it to transfer money to me here. The bank tells me who it would prefer to deal with here, and then I go to the bank in advance to find the individual who will handle the transfer and confirm what identification will be acceptable. In addition, I confirm with my bank what the value date will be. This confirms the date on which the money will be paid out. I then advise my bank to proceed and I have the money the next day.

"As you would expect, wire transfers are very hard to trace. You can walk into a bank in North America and transfer $9,999 without any problem. The reason for the funny number is that the U.S. and Canadian governments want documentation of large transfers. In Europe, you can ask for any amount with no questions. As well, you can transfer a lot of money around using traveller's cheques or bank cheques. For example, if you wanted to move $10,000 without a trace, you could buy the amount in foreign bank traveller's cheques and have them made payable to the recipient at the other end. You don't even have to use your own name when purchasing them. The cashing bank only checks to see if the signatures match. They don't care if the signature is that of Al Zymer or Manuel Labour. Once you put your mind to leaving as small a paper trail as possible, life becomes quite simple."

"This bank you deal with must know that you are using its facilities to beat the tax man. Don't they get upset?" I asked.

"Hold on, Stew. I am avoiding taxes — something that is entirely legal. Although I have a country of record for residence, I in fact have no country of residence, and I provide all my own support systems, from health care to political pork-barrelling. Who do you suggest I pay taxes to on my interest income? It is earned in a country that doesn't charge me taxes on interest earned, and received in a country that does not charge taxes on offshore earnings. Should I volunteer to pay taxes to Mexico? Canada? Japan? Why?"

"Well, Angelo, you've got a point. I guess if the money is earned in a country that doesn't tax it, you shouldn't look for trouble. However, I still feel uneasy about it."

"Let me help you with that. You've heard about the tax-free expense allowances that your MPs and senators have given themselves in Canada, not to mention the free airplane tickets and subsidized meals? Well, I've just done the same. I have credit card accounts that are paid by a corporation. This is my tax-free allowance. I will choose as my final residence a country that has very benign, or no, taxation on foreign earnings. But, right now, I have chosen to have no residence. Therefore, I don't live anywhere and I don't pay taxes anywhere."

"But what about Canada's rule that everyone has to reside somewhere?" I asked.

"I will answer that with the Revenue Canada rule that

says you are resident in the last place you lived. So, I am officially a resident of Holland and receive no benefits from that residency. If they bill me for taxes, I will pay. Remember that income tax is voluntary. You don't have to pay it. It's just that Canada's government gets a little upset if you don't volunteer.

"As for the banks, tax avoidance is a source of revenue for them. They have no morality; no corporation should. Governments provide the moral and legal framework within which we toil. The governments of the countries that assist me in my efforts have no qualms about tax avoidance. Hell, in a number of low-tax jurisdictions, tax evasion isn't even a crime — never mind tax avoidance.

"Why do you think governments like those in the Bahamas, Cayman Islands, Turks and Caicos Islands, Luxembourg, the Isle of Man, and Switzerland have established bank secrecy? These governments are getting rich by helping the overburdened taxpayer get away from it all."

I guess I was still feeling pangs of my liberal guilt and remembrances of my college days' "soak the rich to pay the poor" politics when I said, "If everybody starts avoiding taxes, who will pay for the poor?"

"The government," Ang said.

"Where will it get the money?"

"The government has more than enough money now. As one U.S. researcher pointed out, there are no poor people in the U.S. If you divide the amount of money the U.S. Government allocates for the poor by the number of people below the poverty line, you get a very comfortable level of income. Obviously, as with most government undertakings, the system is inefficient. There is an inability to distribute the funds cheaply. Therefore, much of the money for the poor gets lost in the bureaucracy. Tighten government belts and efficiency will follow.

"As an example of efficiency, look at the old slave system in the American South. There, the slave owners took 100 percent of their workers' output, but were of course liable for all their health and welfare, as a dead or ill worker was a liability. Economists have recently calculated that the net gain to the slave owner was 83 percent, because 17 percent of the output was consumed in maintaining the slave. In our Canadian system, the government requires 40 percent of our output to maintain our health and welfare, and it doesn't even feed us."

I could see what was going on. Angelo had become disgusted with the ever-increasing tax load and the mounting government interference in his life. Instead of complaining, he had taken control of his life, and rather than being dictated to, he called the shots. It was his choice as to what portion of his income he gave up. He had, as well, used commonly available facilities to regain the privacy a person's personal financial matters are due.

It was all starting to fit together but the Cava was taking its toll, and I knew I wanted to remember this. I made some mental notes.

The following were the next steps to be taken after obtaining all my wealth in my hands:

1. Set up an offshore corporation in a country with corporate and bank secrecy.
2. Have the corporation set up a local stock-brokerage account in the jurisdiction with a sub-account in North America.

3. Have the corporation's broker buy securities and register them in the offshore corporate name.
4. Leave instructions with the offshore corporation to transfer interest payments to a bank in a country with bank secrecy.
5. If at all uneasy about the arrangements, obtain insurance on the value of the portfolio.
6. Set up a debit card system with an offshore bank to transfer cash without interest costs.

As I saw the situation, Ang had arranged things so that the bonds were in his hands but registered in someone else's name. The interest was paid into an account into which no one could peek. The interest was transferred to his personal account in a bank located in a country with bank secrecy. He used his debit card to extract $2,000 per month for living expenses. Ang had certainly done his homework. Cute.

No matter how you looked at it, there was going to be a cost item involved, but, as Angelo pointed out, the cost of the avoidance was always less than that of paying taxes. I guess that many high-tax governments have just priced themselves out of the market. The cost of avoidance is significantly less than the cost of taxes.

CHAPTER 6

Laying NEST EGGS

We walked back to the yacht through the streets of Sitges in the early morning. People were just leaving the restaurants.

I thought back to the yummies I had just devoured, but I was still consumed by a hunger for more knowledge. There were still unanswered questions. I knew Angelo had money, but where did it come from? And what about all the support systems in our society, such as health and life insurance?

I tried to broach these with Ang, but he insisted that morning would be a better time to consider these things, when we would be more clear-headed. I knew that the RRSP must have been important, because he went to such ends to move it out of Canada with minimal tax.

The following day was heralded by a beautiful sunny morning. Sarah had made us espresso with their fancy coffee machine. I had thought out my strategy, so I went for the jugular.

"Ang, we, the bridge guys, figured you scored big in the stock market. You worked in the business, you knew what was happening. Mac said it was a number of small scores. The only dissenter was Tim, who says it was real estate."

"No, Stew, none of the above. There is a commonly accepted thesis in investing circles known as 'the efficient market thesis.' This states that all the historical, present, and future prospects of a stock are fully reflected in the share price at any time. Therefore, shares are always fairly priced and there is no opportunity to find a 'winner.'"

"Maybe so, but I see share prices going up and down every day," I said.

"The day-to-day fluctuations in share prices reflect the general attitude toward the market and the economy. There was research done many years ago that showed that something like 65 percent of share price movements reflect investor attitudes toward the market generally. A further 20 percent of share price movements are caused by the attitudes of investors toward the industry in which the company operates. Only 15 percent of share price movements occur as a result of incidents affecting a company specifically. With this in mind, a successful investor is one who can determine market directions rather than pick stocks. After all, what was a great stock to own in Japan when the Nikkei index fell from 39,000 to 18,000? Answer: no stock."

"But I've seen references to 'wealthy market speculators' in publications. How did these people make it?"

"The only people who have managed to beat the market on a continuous basis are those such as Ivan Boesky and David Levine, who dealt with inside information. The efficient-market thesis is so well known by professionals that when they see a constant 'winner,' they immediately become suspicious. Remember Ivan Boesky? He gave up pinstripes for horizontal ones. In my firm, the young guys thought he was a genius, and the old farts wondered when he was going to get caught. There are enough guys in jail for market hanky-panky to start a good-sized brokerage firm."

"Yeah, but I know guys who have scored big on things like Amazon.com. How did they do it?"

"Well, there is no question that they did make some money. However, I remember a comment that was made by a wise, old stock salesman in our office when one of the young fellows was fortunate enough to own shares in a company that found a gold mine. He said to me, 'Young Tomlinson isn't really further ahead. The market has just lent him some money for a while. He will soon give it back.' He did give it back — with interest."

"Ang, you're telling me it is impossible to beat the market. But what about those mutual funds that do so well?"

"If you look at mutual funds in total, you will find that most funds underperform the market indices. By choosing the start and end points of the measurement period to their advantage, most funds can show pretty good, if not spectacular, performance. Mostly, these funds just grow with the general growth of the market. That is why there are 'index funds,' which invest in a basket of stocks mirroring the market indices. They will never over- or underperform the market, but have the advantage of management fees that are in the .7-percent area, rather than the 2.5 percent paid on actively managed funds. There are many pension funds that see this as a way to invest in the country's economy without tears or brokerage expenses. This also gets past the psychological problem in the market."

"What do you mean by 'psychological problem'?" I asked.

"As you know, Stew, some people are optimists, others pessimists. There is nobody who does not have a bias one way or the other. Most portfolio managers are optimists, believing that the market will always go up. Over the long term, they are right, but it is those short-term market disasters that hurt. Obviously, during a bull market, the best performance is going to be in the current fad stocks. There have been times when it was the 'conglomerates,' at other times the 'concept' stocks. These were then followed by the dot-com mania. The players pay obscene prices for the fad stock of the moment. However, when the dance ends and the market falls, it is these stocks that suffer the most. The optimists own the fad stocks and have great performance at the top of the market. At the height of a bull market, it is the portfolio manager with the most fad stocks who is the clear winner. When the market falls, the portfolios of the extreme optimists show the greatest declines. They can never beat the market because they are always fully invested, believing in the perpetuity of the bull market and their own infallibility. An old friend of mine had a wonderful plaque on his desk with the inscription 'Don't confuse intelligence with a bull market.'"

"You, a stock-market professional, are telling me I'll never score big in the market and that I should own an index fund?"

"Better yet, set up your own index fund by buying the

top ten weighted stocks in the Standard & Poor's 500 or the Toronto Stock Exchange's index. The top ten in Toronto represent more than 70 percent of the total value of the exchange. The reason I specified ten stocks is because with that number of companies in your portfolio, you will have 85 percent of the effects of diversification. As you know, holding one stock can be both risky and highly rewarding. Increasing the number of companies in your portfolio diminishes your risk from single-event problems."

"How well will I do?"

"The value of the U.S. stock markets, on a long-term basis — and I am talking 30 years — has shown about 6-percent* real compound annual growth. This outpaces GNP, but is close to the rate of growth of the index of industrial production.

"As you know, during our bridge games, when you guys would ask me for a hot tip, I would always say Bell Phone and everybody would laugh. I meant it. I always advised you fellows not to trade stocks in your RRSPs but to buy and hold. Your RRSPs couldn't afford the brokerage and transfer fees."

I then thought of the big score my nephew had made in Goliath, a penny gold-mining stock that he bought for $2.50 and sold for $28. I was sure I could corner Ang with a question.

---

* The 6 percent is an interesting number because the long-term apparent growth (which includes inflation) has been between 10 and 11 percent. This indicates a long-term inflation rate of between 4 and 5 percent. The long-term real return on bonds (ex-inflation) has been 4 percent. The higher 2-percent yield of stocks over bonds is attributed by students of the market as reward for the higher risk of stocks.

"Ang, remember my nephew Sandy? He bought Goliath for $2.50 and sold it for $28. Obviously he made lots of money in the market. How do you explain that?"

"How many times has he increased his capital? Tenfold? To win at mining speculation, he would have to make at least 140 times his investment."

"How do you come up with that figure?"

"Cominco, the large successful mining company, kept records on its exploration efforts. It reported that, between 1929 and 1969, it had expended $300 million on mining exploration. Cominco had examined 1,000 properties, of which it took fewer than 68 to extensive exploration. Of those extensively explored properties, only seven returned their original investment or made money. That's a success ratio of 1 in 143. Too bad for Sandy, he's going to continue betting on the penny stocks, trying to beat the 143 to 1 odds again, until all his winnings are gone."

"Well, who does make money in the stock market? The brokers?" I asked.

"Yes, Stew, those fancy houses owned by the stock salesmen are a testament to that, but it all comes from commission income and their ownership or participation in their firms. They are just like any other professionals earning an income. If I am not mistaken, your stockbroker is about 60 years old. Why isn't he retired on the yacht next to mine? If he has such great insight into the market, why is he still working? Why are any of them working after age 40? If they have such good information for you, why don't they utilize it themselves and make a fortune?"

I was supposed to be asking the questions, but Ang had me thinking — something I am loath to do when it comes to my own circumstances. He was obviously right. Like the

tourist in New York who was shown the stockbrokers'
yachts in the East River and was erudite enough to ask
where the clients' yachts were, the light dawned on me. I
remembered the wag's comment that a stockbroker was a
person who invested your money until it was all gone.

It was now obvious: a fast, tax-free killing in the stock
market for my RRSP was not in the cards. Then, like a message from on high, it struck me. I now knew why the
government had changed the tax laws to allow capital
losses to be charged only against prior capital gains and not
against earned income. The old system was too costly, as all
the suckers blew their brains out in the market and then
charged the losses against their income for tax purposes.
Geez, I had $20,000 in losses I might never offset with
gains. Under the old system, the taxman could kiss $5,000
goodbye.*

The sun was at its zenith and Sarah had just returned
from the market with, of all things, fresh produce, and I
could see a bottle of Rioja sticking out of one of the bags.
In a single day, I had become enough of an authority on
Spanish wines to know that Rioja is the good stuff. You can
see where my priorities are; my wife would sell the kids
into slavery for really fresh produce in November, rather
than stomach the eight-day-old California lettuce we end
up with in Toronto.

Sarah made a salad that contained, as well as a variety

---

* When first instituted in Canada, only 50 percent of capital gains
were taxed and, at the time, the top marginal rate was 50 percent.
Therefore, 50 percent of Stew's capital loss ($10,000) would have
been eligible for tax treatment and would have given rise to tax relief
at the marginal rate of 50 percent, or $5,000.

of lettuces, some sort of cold beans about the size of small marbles, anchovies, and tuna. It was served with bread still warm from the bakery, extra-virgin olive oil, and copious amounts of Rioja. Sarah informed me that all of Spain shuts down between one o'clock and five o'clock, and we were about to do the same. Sarah and Ang moved into their spacious forward cabin, and I stretched out in the cockpit to finish *The Economist* that I had bought to read on the plane.

I couldn't get into *The Economist*. I tried starting at the back, reading the book reviews, then moving to the finance section. I kept thinking back to what Angelo had told me about the stock market and I was struck by several insights. I now understood why they called it a stock exchange. It was where people came to exchange their shares. These represented ownership of a corporation. This differed from the other financial arenas, such as the futures markets, where people bought and sold contracts for the delivery of anything from dollars to pork bellies. In other words, they placed bets on the direction of prices. If a share was always fairly priced, how could anyone make a fortune? I knew of people who had become rich from their share holdings, but it seemed they were all in jail for insider trading or rigging markets.

As I dozed off, I hoped I would remember the following:

1. Stock markets were not developed to help long-suffering wage slaves get rich fast.
2. Stock markets are probably the most price-efficient mechanisms in the world.
3. The stock market consists of hundreds of thousands

of individuals who, in their collective wisdom, determine the price of a share. Those who think they are
going to outperform that immense pool of intellect
are suffering from terminal vanity.

I drifted off, gazing up at the hole in the ozone layer,
with the Chinese restaurant syndrome still nagging at me.
I was unsatisfied. Ang had gone to a lot of trouble to move
that RRSP out of the country with minimal tax. It must
have been worth more than a few bucks. How did it get
that way? When Angelo started investing, you could put in
a maximum of only $5,500 per year. I had to know more.
A passing boat created just enough wake to rock me to
sleep.

I awoke to see Ang playing captain, as he puttered
around checking battery condition and bilge levels. I was
beginning to feel guilty about taking a free course in finance,
but my curiosity had gotten the best of me. I still couldn't
fathom the reality of a 50-year-old man sitting on a more-
than-one-quarter-million-dollar-yacht, who only months
ago had finally broken the $100,000-per-year salary level.

My host asked me to help him with some chores on
deck. We were running some new lines to replace those
that had worn down during his crossing of the Atlantic.
There was another subject I wanted to ask about. I was
wondering if two weeks was going to be enough. I thought
I'd better get back to the inquisition or I would soon run
out of time. I figured I'd better find the source of his
wealth and leisure before it was too late.

As I carried a line back to the cockpit, I threw out the
bait to Ang.

"Ang, Tim says the money came from real estate." Tim

was one of the bridge foursome who was forever trading houses and always moving up in price and size.

"In a way he is right, Stew. As you know, I lived close to my office and either walked or took public transport to work. I didn't own a car, and Sarah and I would often comment about the $5,000 annual dividend we received from General Motors. Of course, what we really meant was the annual after-tax savings we incurred by not owning a vehicle. This was offset by our taxi and limousine bills, which came to about $1,800 per year. I remember how, during those years, I would roll in from a party in a taxi or limo and hope I could make it from the curb to my stairs without someone stepping on my knuckles. Just imagine 20 years of partying and not one drunk driving charge. Twenty years of shopping and no parking tickets."

"Ang, aren't cars really a convenience rather than an expense?"

"If you want to really have convenience with a car, you need to be able to park it once you arrive at your destination. There are only two ways you can guarantee this. One is to use the system used by off-duty police officers, who put a piece of police clothing on their dashboard or rear platform. This allows them to park anywhere without a ticket. All you have to do is obtain a police rain-jacket or other article of clothing. The tough part is getting the garment. It's worth a lot. The other method is easier.

"Arrange to get one of those licence plates reserved for the handicapped. A lot of my friends have them. They either registered the car in the name of an invalid relative or got the documentation they needed from a well-placed friend. It was amusing to see all those big Mercedes, Cadillacs, and BMWs with handicapped stickers parked in the no-parking zone of the opera house front door. Their owners would run from the hall at the end of a performance to avoid the traffic. Some invalids! Must I say more?"

"So you are saying that car ownership is expensive, impoverishing, and inconvenient?"

"Stew, it's not only the actual car but all the other incidental expenses. Even traffic law is set up not so much as a method of maintaining order but as a system to generate revenue."

"Yeah, I guess you're right. Otherwise, they would tow away illegally parked cars rather than put tickets on them. Towing would solve the problem, but it would also discourage the offence and hence the revenue it creates. So, ditch the car and you save $5,000."

"Actually, closer to $10,000 pre-tax and $5,000 after tax."

"So, you always bought houses close to your office?"

"No, I only owned the one house. I never traded. After all, the real-estate market is an auction market like the stock market and is therefore efficient. Nobody wins or loses in an efficient market."

"Ang, you mean to say that you could not have made more by trading?"

"Well, Stew, remember my cousin Luigi? He started off by buying a $100,000 house in York Mills, Ontario, about 20 years ago, and has since bought and sold three other houses, the last one for a million dollars. The original York Mills house that Luigi purchased and sold would today be worth $500,000. If you subtract that $500,000 from the one million dollars Luigi received on the sale of his last home, it would appear he has netted $500,000. However, I figure that, all told, he has paid $100,000 in real-estate commissions, not to mention legal expenses and transfer fees. Thus, you might say all that trading over the 20 years netted him $400,000. Again, not so. He has also paid a lot of interest, moving fees, and redecoration costs. I would estimate that in reality he made about $100,000 to $150,000 by trading."

"Hey, Ang, that's not to be sneezed at! Also, it's tax free."

"First, if he had invested $22,000 at 10 percent in an RRSP for his wife, or used some of the many income-splitting forms, such as a children's or inter vivos trust, that were available 20 years ago, by now it would have been worth $150,000. Second, I am going to make a great prophecy. Before you retire, Stew, the capital gains on a principal residence will become taxable in some form or other."

"Yeah, that's a safe bet, Ang. You don't have to be a genius to see it coming. First, it was taking away the second family home as a tax break. Prior to 1982, a husband and wife were each entitled to have a principal residence and thereby realize any gains on the sale of either property tax free. The government realized that it was missing out on millions of dollars and changed the legislation in 1982. Spouses are now permitted to have only one principal residence between them. Soon, it will be the capital gains exemptions for small business shares, farm property, and the one principal residence. I bet I know how the government will do it. It will use the old 'let's tax the rich' ploy. It will introduce the tax only on gains on houses selling for over $500,000, and then wait for inflation and government-induced housing shortages to move the price of a dump up to the $500,000 level."

"Actually, Stew, if you look at the February 1992 budget,

part of that is already under way. The government that Pierre Trudeau took out of the nation's bedrooms was put back by Brian Mulroney. The Mulroney government decided that, for tax purposes, people who sleep together too often are married. Therefore, only one of them is allowed the principal residence exemption."

"Wait a minute," I said. "I didn't notice that piece of legislation. Can you explain that a little further?"

"The Canadian government has now proclaimed that, for tax purposes, people living common law will be subjected to the same tax treatment as married couples, and therefore must give up the benefits of single status. So, with a stroke of the pen, people who had no intention of forming a permanent relationship were forced into one."

"That seems rather draconian. Is this a reflection of desperation?" I asked.

"Very much so, Stew. You see, governments, like all institutions, have as their first objective their own self-preservation."

Angelo was confusing me. I had always believed that institutions were set up to serve some function. I asked if this were not true.

"Of course, in the first instance, an institution comes into existence to serve some need in society. But what happens when that need no longer exists? Did Greenpeace close its doors once nuclear testing had ceased? No, it went on to whales and now trees. I remember first becoming aware of such institutional self-preservation from the mining analyst at my old firm.

"He had just returned from a trip to England to talk to clients and we were having our morning meeting. The price of silver was about $35 per ounce and appeared to be headed higher. We knew that Bunker Hunt had cornered the market and he was squeezing the short sellers.* We knew there were problems because many of the short sellers were floor traders, and hence professionals, and they were screaming bloody blue murder. We were trying to find a way to profit from the situation when the mining analyst reminded us of how, in 1923, a speculator, a Frenchman, with the aid of the old Banque Nationale de Paris, had cornered the copper market on the London Metal Exchange. The price of copper was going through the roof and the professionals, who had sold short, were being badly burned. Rather than see the market devastated, the governors of the London Metal Exchange changed the rules regarding what constituted good delivery against contracts, thus allowing the fulfilling of short sales with material that previously was not considered acceptable. The price collapsed, as did the bank, and the speculator killed himself. Our mining analyst warned us that if things got too difficult for the traders, the commodities exchange in the U.S. would change the rules regarding silver to save itself and its professionals. As you know, that's exactly what it did."

"I don't get what this has to do with governments," I said.

---

* Short sellers are speculators who expect the price of a commodity to fall. They sell material they don't own at current prices with the anticipation of buying it in the future at a lower price. If the buyer of the non-existent material demands delivery, the short seller has a problem if there is none to be borrowed to give to the buyer who is demanding delivery. In the extreme case, the short seller has to buy, in the open market, irrespective of price, material to fulfill his contract.

"The government is an institution. Its first objective is to preserve itself. Therefore, we still have capital punishment in Canada."

"You're mistaken there," I said. "We don't have capital punishment in Canada."

"Not so, Stew. If someone kills your Aunt Agatha in cold blood, the murderer will not be executed. But if that same person commits treason, the traitor will be hanged. It's all right for your Aunt Agatha to die a horrible death, but not the state. The state does not strive to protect your Aunt Agatha from some crazed junkie because the state is also a junkie.

"Money is the opium of the state. But like all junkies, it needs constantly bigger fixes. The bureaucrats are aware of the laws of diminishing returns with regard to taxation. They have come to the limit of what people will bear in Canada. Now, rather than direct rate increases for income taxes, ways of broadening the net have to be undertaken. Hence, a forthcoming tax on housing. The junkie must be saved no matter how inequitable the course taken to achieve that end."

"Okay. But tell me: the house is supposed to be the most important asset in any family. How does that fit into your scheme of things?"

"First of all, treat the house like what it is: an asset. Don't buy frivolously so that the house becomes a major ongoing cash drain. Buy in such a way as to minimize your living costs. Remember that if you buy in the country and you work in town, you will need two cars: one for you and one for your wife. When your children mature, they too will need cars. Auto-mobiles are a depreciating asset. Instead of paying for travel costs, live close to your daily activities.

Then, use the saved transportation expenditures to increase the principal amount of your monthly mortgage payment on your house, which is a non-depreciating asset. After all, you don't see farmers living downtown and commuting to their farms. All those extra expenses are paid with after-tax dollars. The sooner the house is paid off, the sooner you will have low-cost accommodation. If you live close to your work, you will also increase your free time (you'll spend less time travelling back and forth to work).

"Whenever you expend money on the house, upgrade. Don't replace a cheap fence with another cheap fence. Make a substantial capital investment in your asset so that you don't have to continue pouring money into it. You know those classy girls from the private schools that your son goes out with?"

"Yeah, what about them?"

"Well, the reason they always look so well dressed is that instead of having a lot of cheap clothes, they have a few top- quality outfits that always look 'rich.' The wealthy can't afford to buy cheap things over and over again. But the poor always do and therefore remain poor. Seeing as how you don't intend to trade the house, you can put the very best fixtures and appliances in it, and avoid the continual need to replace or repair. An $800 dishwasher over the long haul is cheaper than the $400 one."

"I see what you're getting at, Ang. When making capital investments in your house, always buy top-of-the-line equipment. If you intend to keep the house, you will have the use of the purchases for a good many years, but if you trade the house, you'll never get paid for them. Another good reason to buy and hold. In fact, a successful stockbroker once gave me the very same advice about blue chip stocks. I guess a house can be compared to a blue chip stock."

"In more ways than you think. Use your house as a capital asset. Because your house is valuable, any equity you build in the house is bankable. In fact, you should move all of your business borrowing onto the house. Let me explain.

"When I left my old firm 15 years ago, I had built up a small equity stake, which I sold back to the firm. I immediately used this money to pay down my mortgage. When I moved to the new firm, I needed capital to buy into it. I borrowed money from the bank using the house as collateral. My loans outstanding at the bank were once again back to their old levels, but now part of the money I owed was considered a business loan, and the interest I paid was tax deductible. Whenever I received a bonus or payout from my firm, I applied it against the outstanding house mortgage and left the business loan outstanding."

"Ang, what you're saying is that every time I have extra money, I should use it to pay down my mortgage and then use the house as collateral* for any business loan I need, right?"

"Partially. To really maximize the use of your assets, set up situations where you can reduce the mortgage and increase the business loan."

"Wow, the folks at Revenue Canada must hate that ploy. Can't they stop you?"

"No, Stew. When you receive an after-tax payment, such as a bonus, pay your after-tax obligations, such as a home mortgage, but leave your pre-tax business obligations

---

* It is important that the loan be set up by the banker as separate from the mortgage to ensure the deductibility of the interest. If necessary, different banks should be used for each loan.

outstanding. You are allowed to do that as a result of the Canadian court case I mentioned earlier that, in 1938, went to the House of Lords in England. At the time, that was the highest court for Canadian appeals. The lords decided that a man had the right to arrange his business affairs in such a way as to minimize his tax liability. That, of course, infuriates the tax officials. They can't get by that decision. But what they have done is to bring into law a rule that if you undertake a transaction that has no other effect than to lower your tax liability, then the tax benefits will not be forthcoming. This, of course, opens a Pandora's box. It brings into question the selling of stock market losers to offset capital gains at year end."

"If I understand you, the general rule is buy the most expensive house you can afford and hold on to it."

"Not quite. The 'hold on' is correct," Ang said, "but remember that a house is an asset with a utility function. It should be bought with its usefulness end cost in mind. The cost should reflect its utility in the same way you bankers value companies on the basis of price as a multiple of sales or earnings."

"What is the price-earnings multiple* of a house?" I asked.

"When you value a building for a loan by the bank, how do you determine what it's worth? Isn't one of the criteria

---

* Stock-market investors will divide the current market price of a share by the most recent 12 months' earnings per share or the expected future 12 months' earnings. They then compare these to the equivalent numbers for the market generally. This gives an indication of the validity of the share price. This ratio of price divided by earnings is the often quoted price-earnings (PE) ratio or multiple.

the amount of annual rent it brings in? Look at my old house, which I sold for $350,000. It would rent for $1,600 per month, or $19,200 per year. To rent the house for $19,200 per year, I would have to earn $38,400 pre-tax. That amount of earnings could be produced by $384,000 of capital invested at 10 percent. Look at the following calculation:

RESIDENCE CAPITAL REQUIREMENTS

	Own	Rent
Purchase Capital Required	$350,000	
Expense Capital Required*	$71,000	
Rent Generating Capital		$384,000
Total Capital Required	$421,000	$384,000

"With interest rates at 10 percent, as a renter, I would need to invest $384,000 to generate enough revenue to cover my occupancy cost. An owner has to put up a $421,000 investment to live in the house. What does that tell you?"

"As a banker, I can tell you that either the price is too high or the rent is too low," I said.

"Ang, it tells me that, as an investment, the house has $37,000 ($421,000–$384,000) of 'fluff' in it. If rental rates go up in the future, or if the house appreciates in value, you might be able to make a decent return, but I wouldn't bet on it. Remember, expenses will also increase."

"Are you saying, Ang, that I can't expect to get any real

* An owner would have to invest sufficient capital to generate a further $7,100 interest before tax, or $3,550 annually after tax, to cover the property taxes, insurance, and repairs. Generating this $7,100 will require an additional $71,000 of capital.

appreciation annually in my house?"

"Good question. Let's look at history. In downtown Toronto, houses were trading hands at $3,300 in 1929, a boom year. If you consider raw, renovatable product as equivalent to a 60-year-old house and look at prices in 1989, you would find that the same house would sell for around $200,000. That would give you an annual appreciation of 7 percent over the 60 years from boom to boom."

"I noticed that you were careful to pick boom periods. Is there something you are trying to tell me?" I asked.

"I was trying to keep the comparisons equivalent. In that 60-year period, there were times when you could have bought a very nice downtown home for under $1,000."

"Wow, that's a deal! How do you think a bond investment would have performed over that 60-year period?" I asked.

"That's tough to answer, Stew. You see, during that period, government bond issues yielded anywhere from 4 to 14 percent. My gut feeling is that a bond fund, at worst, would have matched the real-estate appreciation."

"What you are telling me is that I shouldn't own a house."

"Not really. I'm just playing the devil's advocate and trying to point out to you that it is not, at this time, the great investment people talk it up to be. You should buy sensibly and not put too much of your wealth into a house because it does cost you more than renting. The real economic picture remains murky because of the weird tax status of a principal residence. If the government were to take away some of the tax breaks, home ownership could become a real burden.

"Think of some of the continents other than North

America. In Europe, the most common form of occupancy is rental accommodation. In all cases where renting is more popular than owning, it is because of the financial structure of occupancy. In France, the most advantageous after-tax residence is rented, not owned. People are selfish. They usually take whatever economic course is most beneficial to them."

"But my parents always said that residential rental properties were a great investment," I said.

"They were, right after World War II. Many immigrants who came to this country in those years saved their money to buy a property to rent. The fellow I bought my house from was just such a man. He tried to have me buy another property he owned, a rooming house on Berkeley Street. I needed $5,000 down, or 10 percent of the purchase price, and the rents would have covered all the costs, including taxes and insurance, while throwing off $100 per month. On the original investment, the annual yield would have been 24 percent pre-tax or 12 percent after tax. A year later, a speculator offered him $75,000. With a 10-percent down payment of $7,500, the return had fallen to 16 percent pre-tax and 8 percent after tax. The old fellow didn't consider the risk and effort worthwhile, and chose to sell and park his money elsewhere. The increasing capital costs of his product — rental properties — had driven him out of the rental business."

"Why buy a house at all, Ang, if it doesn't make sense financially?"

"A house, first of all, is a great forced-savings program. Every month, in the form of repayment of capital, you increase your net worth. Second, you can have insured tenancy. You can't be kicked out. Third, you arrange the dwelling to your style and taste. Fourth, you have an automatic inflation hedge, which springs into action at the first sign of government-induced inflation. Finally, you have an asset that you can collateralize at inflated values. Remember, the bank will be willing to lend on the basis of the higher potential sales value, not on its lower financial or economic value, unless they have learned from the Olympia and York debacle."

I felt another insight coming on. As a banker, I worked for years on leasing projects where assets were sold to the bank's leasing company and rented back to the original owners at a rate that would cover the financial and capital costs. I could not understand how the savings and loan operations in the U.S. had managed to get into bad residential real-estate loans and eventual bankruptcy. I thought there could never be such a thing as a bad residential real-estate loan. After all, if the lenders couldn't get their money from the owner, then they should foreclose and rent out the property to recover the loan. Therein lies the rub. With the bizarre real-estate prices in North America, you cannot buy a house and rent it to cover your costs. The prices are far beyond the economic value of the property. I had never considered the situation where the purchase price of a house was far in excess of its financial or economic value.

Well, Ang had tricked me again. While he had me engrossed in all this financial chatter, I had assisted in the replacement of the jib sheets and main halyard without noticing. I guess my host felt guilty because he suggested we stop our chores and have a sundowner. I realized he still had not answered my question as to the source of his money. Was I to spend another day working on his boat just to extract a simple truth? Well, why not? I had picked up a number of good ideas as far as maximizing my savings, and had learned some new knots in the bargain. Now, it was just a matter of remembering to:

1. Reduce my operating costs by lowering or eliminating my daily travel expenses.
2. Settle in a house that I could live in for a long stretch and avoid trading, no matter what my wife says.
3. Always upgrade with the best of fixtures and appliances so as to reduce my maintenance costs.
4. Build up equity in the house as fast as possible to eliminate the non-tax-deductible real-estate interest and replace it, wherever possible, with tax-deductible business interest.
5. Recognize that there is an inherent hidden financial cost to house ownership versus renting and budget for this. Once I own my house, I am not going to buy a more expensive one and increase my hidden costs.

CHAPTER 7

Your Pension Will Be Indexed
WHEN THIS BOOK IS

By now, I had reduced the number of possibilities for the source of Ang's independence. I knew a number of people who had worked for Bell Canada and IBM and who had retired very well, which led me to believe that Ang's pension was obviously a big part of his independence.

"Ang," I said, "you must have had a great pension fund to retire this well."

Ang chuckled. "Yeah, unfortunately, the government is doing everything it can to reduce my defined-benefit pension to nothing before it goes bankrupt."

I knew a bit about pensions from my friends at the bank, but I wasn't sure what Ang meant by a defined-benefit pension. "What do you mean by defined benefit?" I asked.

"Well, it's one of the two basic types of pension. You make a monthly fixed contribution, and when you retire or move on, the company's pension-fund administrators pay your share of the fund's earnings to you."

"It would seem to me, Ang, that under that sort of scheme you would never know how much you were going to get at the end of the day."

"Correct, but you always get your fair share."

"What do you mean by 'you get your fair share'?"

"Well, when you leave the plan, the plan's administrators determine the total value of the investments on the departure day and pay your share in dollars into another plan or purchase an annuity for you."

"That seems fair enough to me, but why was there such a fuss back in the mid-1980s from the unions about pensions?"

"Well, Stew, if you think back to those days, you will remember that the stock market was at full boil. Every day, the business papers carried growing lists of share prices reaching new all-time highs."

"Yeah, great times in my business," I said.

"Well, the unions discovered that the pension funds of their employers had made tremendous profits, but the future pensioners were not going to benefit from those profits."

"That doesn't seem fair, Ang. How did that arise?"

"The employers had set up defined-benefit programs for their employees. This meant that, irrespective of the earnings of the plans, the employees were guaranteed a certain fixed income upon retirement — even if the fund had not been successful in its investments and did not have sufficient funds to pay that income."

"Where would the money come from to cover the shortfall?"

"The company would have had to provide the difference, Stew. However, if the investments of the pension funds did very well and exceeded the requirements to pay the pensioners, then the company would keep the excess."

"Ang, if the companies were taking out the difference between the payout requirements and the funds' earnings, where did the unions get the idea that the pension funds contained excess funds that rightly belonged to the pensioners?"

"That's just the problem, Stew. The companies left all the money in the pension plans. This allowed the companies to avoid paying income tax on the excess. The other advantage, for the companies, was that if the pension fund had a bad investment year, the employer would not have to put up additional funds. The excess would take care of the required funding. Also, in bad times, when corporate earnings were low, the companies could dip into their pension excesses to bolster their cash flows. They could also avoid making the required annual contribution, using instead the previous year's surpluses to meet current funding obligations. As you can see, it gave the companies a lot of flexibility."

"Why would an employee even agree to a plan like this?"

"Most of these plans were set up during the depression of the 1930s as a way to keep key employees from leaving their jobs. The plan was a perk to the employee, and many employees recognized that with the poor investment climate, there was little benefit to be gained by sharing in investments that might never appreciate. Therefore, the best pension plan was one that guaranteed the worker a fixed income upon retirement."

"Obviously, those plans aren't as popular today, are they, Ang?"

"They will be if we enter a prolonged economic recession.* But remember, they are the most conservative of plans because of the guaranteed aspect. As people grow older and more conservative, they recognize the benefit of having a fixed guaranteed income to look forward to. Also, these plans usually base the payout on an average of the employee's best years of earnings, which is attractive."

"One thing that strikes me as odd is that there was never a hue and cry about over-funding in the Canada Pension Plan," I said.

"That's because the CPP was funded only in spirit. The government sold its bonds to the fund at high prices and hence low yields. In other words, your CPP dollars were used to finance current government spending. Can you imagine relying on the performance of a low-yield bond fund to provide retirement income? As things currently stand, the CPP is paying out about $500 million net of what it collects annually and has $49 billion in assets. Regrettably, its obligations come to $600 billion. Obviously, it is under-funded. The government has taken to investing in more real securities, but the problem will be difficult to solve. The asset base would have to grow at 13 percent annually to meet its obligations. That assumes the half-billion-dollar net outflow stops immediately. When you consider that the fastest-growing stock market in the world over the past century was the U.S. market at 6 per-

---

* A perfect storm has hit some U.S. pension plans in that corporate sponsors such as airlines and car companies may go bankrupt being unable to pay the defined benefits promised to pensioners.

cent, it is unlikely that the CPP will reach its funding requirements through the efforts of its investment managers. They would have to be magicians to achieve 13 percent growth in a 6-percent market. Yes, you can bet the feds are constantly looking for some way to get out of paying CPP to all those who have paid into it."

"How can they do that, Ang? They've contracted with the contributors to the plan to pay them."

"Oh, they'll pay them all right. However, like the Old Age Security, they will find a way to tax it all back."

"I don't mind the Old Age Security being taxed back, but not my CPP. The Old Age Security is paid out of general revenues, while the CPP is a return of my own premiums."

"You should also be incensed that the Old Age Security is being taxed back. The Old Age Security was started in 1952 as a program to ensure that all Canadians had pensions. It was an unfunded 'pay as you go' fund, with everyone paying a 2 percent tax that went into a fund called the Old Age Security Revenue Fund. It was a progressive tax, meaning the more you earned, the more you paid. In 1972, the tax rate was increased to 4 percent and was included within the general tax rate. In 1975, the skulduggery began. With a simple transfer, the government shifted the Old Age Security Revenue Fund into the Consolidated Revenue Fund. The pension pool that people had paid their tax dollars into disappeared, with the money ending up in the government's coffers. However, at that particular time, the government recognized their social contract and vowed to keep the faith. The pensioners would always be able to get back what they paid in. Sort of."

"Ang, are you telling me that the government is actually taxing back, from current retirees, money that was put aside from a special tax originally levied to give Canadians pensions?"

"Yup. I call it Maxwellization, after Robert Maxwell."

"Who is Robert Maxwell?" I asked.

"Actually, 'was' is the better verb. Robert Maxwell is no more. He was the controlling shareholder and managing director of the Mirror Newspaper Group. He concluded that many of his company's pensioners were receiving pensions that were much too generous. Undoubtedly, some of the pensioners were doing quite well as a result of their private savings and the generous pension benefits obtained by the printer's union in the U.K. To alleviate the problem of excessive payments to his pensioners, Robert Maxwell converted their savings to his own use, believing that he was better equipped to handle the lifestyle of fancy yachts and expensive villas. When it became apparent that his house of cards was about to collapse, he jumped off his yacht near the Canary Islands and drowned. The U.K. government has since enacted a series of pension reforms to stop any further theft of pension funds."

"Well, thank God Robert Maxwell is gone and the private-sector rape of pensions is over. What about the Old Age Security system, does it also have a happy ending?"

"No. Even today, 4 percent of your tax dollars goes to fund Old Age Security. Can you imagine the howls that would have been heard in 1972 if the government had said it was imposing a 4-percent income tax for pensions, but only the poor would receive the pensions? We are talking serious discrimination here. Why should anyone work if the pension is guaranteed only if you earned less than $50,000? To guarantee your piece of the pie, you'd have to goof off."

"This is all starting to sound vaguely dishonest," I said.

"Vaguely? Get serious, Stew. Suppose General Motors' executives gave themselves big benefits, handed out high-paying, do-nothing jobs to their friends, threw lavish parties, and declared big dividends to all shareholders, only to later find out that they were a little short to balance the budget and, therefore, had to roll the employees' pension fund into general operating revenue. The government would proceed to exchange the executives' pinstripes for horizontal jail stripes.

"Now, think back, Stew. What was special about the year 1975?"

"I can't think of anything."

"It was a special year in Canada because it was the first time since the end of World War II that the government's annual deficit exceeded 3 percent of the gross domestic product. This benchmark of 3 percent of gross domestic product is a commonly accepted yardstick of good fiscal management for government. However, the mandarins found a way to get the politicians off the hook. They simply rolled the taxpayers' pension funds into the general coffers, thereby increasing the level of government funds. Mind you, our friends in Ottawa were quick to point out that this was just to tidy the bookkeeping and that no one would be adversely affected. You will note that this promise lasted all of 18 years. Now, they want to tax back the 4 percent paid in by anyone who earns more than $50,000. Not surprisingly, the MPs did not suggest that they would also tax back a portion of the amount that their pensions exceeded $50,000.

"The politicians have trotted out the old 'soak the rich to pay the poor' song and dance, but this is different. Suppose you deposited $200 in your bank every week while your spendthrift brother paid $200 a week for a lease on a Porsche. At the end of the year, the banker says your balance is too high and proceeds to give a portion of your account to your brother. The message seems to be live high on the hog and let the other guy pay for it. If the Old Age Security system isn't sacrosanct, then how can you be sure of the CPP?

"With the MPs and their friends taking so much of the pension pie, there won't be enough of the CPP to go around. The next step will be to take away a portion of the CPP from Canadians to be sure that there is enough to pay the pensions of the MPs. I have it from reliable sources that the CPP will be means-tested in 2010 or shortly thereafter.

"I guess I kind of rattled on there, Stew, but I always get on my soapbox when I see the big guys taking the little guys for a ride. For years, the politicians and bureaucrats have managed to convince the people that the thieves in their midst are the corporations. Meanwhile, Ottawa has ripped off the people's pension funds."

"From the appearance of your lifestyle, I can see they didn't rip you off, Ang," I said. "You must have had a great defined-contribution or -benefit plan to pay for this lifestyle."

"Stew, I guess I kind of fell into the best. At the time, I didn't realize when I started my RRSP that I was embarking on a defined-contribution plan, while my employers continued with their defined-benefit plans."

At that moment, I finally realized the difference between defined-benefit and defined-contribution plans, but how many other people did? Obviously, many union leaders didn't. Of course, they had a point that the companies had made profits on the contributions of the employees, who were only entitled to a fixed benefit and not the gains. However, they had not thought of the other side of the question: what if there were losses? Suppose the investment managers had lost money on the employee contributions. Were the employees going to be required to top up the pension fund? Not bloody likely. Regrettably, the trauma of the 1930s depression is no longer remembered. Everybody wanted the defined-benefit pension in that period of deflation. It seemed to me that the only fair proposition was a pension with a fixed benefit indexed to inflation. The only people who get those are the privilegentia of government. The closest thing a poor working Canadian would ever get to an indexed pension was a good RRSP, but how could someone assume a good RRSP?

Ang's words were echoing in my head, and all I could think about was how someone could get a good RRSP. My mind quickly turned to thoughts of Angelo and this lovely boat I was on.

"Yeah," I said, "but nobody makes money in their RRSPs."

Ang retorted, "Not so. I and many others have made excellent money in RRSPs."

I thought about my own RRSP. The statements from my broker showed that ten years of gains had been wiped out in the dot-com frenzy. I thought I'd better pursue this further, since I did have another ten years to try and make it back.

For the first time in my life, I really thought about my various pensions. How different from the days of my youth when I didn't even ask if my employers sponsored one. Now I made a mental note that when I got back to Toronto, I was going to find out exactly what type of pension funds I had participated in over the years with various employers and what I had coming to me. I remembered that when I left my previous employer, a portion of my pension had been "locked in." What this meant was that my employer's portion could not be taken out before I reached age 65. The funds rested with my trust company and were administered by me, but were in a separate account. This meant I had to pay two administration fees, one for my normal plan and one for the locked-in plan. So what were the questions I would have to ask? They were as follows:

1. What type of plan had I been enrolled in?
2. If it was a defined-benefit plan, what were the terms?
3. What options did I have to increase my annual contribution?
4. How well were the various pension-fund managers performing?
5. Could I consolidate any of my plans in order to reduce my fees?

"Ang," I asked, "how can you make money in your RRSP?"

"First and foremost," Ang said, "save money."

"I don't understand. I thought an RRSP was a savings plan."

"Stew, the word 'saving' has two meanings; it means 'to hold on to or acquire' but it also means 'to be thrifty and not spend wantonly.' I am talking about being cheap in your RRSP and not spending money foolishly. There are a number of things that you must and must not do in order to save money in your self-administered pension plan.

"First, don't trade. Remember that every transaction requires the payment of a commission to your broker, as well as the cost of registration of the new securities and the consequent reduction of the size of your fund. Instead, find a security you can be happy with, preferably until the day you cash in your plan, and hold it. Sell the security only if you are firmly convinced that the company will no longer be able to grow at the rate you originally thought attainable on a long-term basis. Don't expect a company to perform well in a recession; therefore, don't look at the company's performance in the short term. When I bought something for my RRSP, it was to hold until the bitter end."

"But, Ang, if you know the market is going down, why not sell out and then buy back just before it turns around?"

"Stew, that is really naive. Do you think they ring a bell on the floor of the exchange when the market is about to turn?"

"Of course not," I said. "But there must be signs, aren't there? What about the economy and a turnaround?"

"First of all, the market does not move in step with economic cycles but anticipates events somewhere between four and nine months in the future. As well, the stock market has, as the saying goes, 'anticipated and reacted to seven of the last four recessions.' Believe me, you are not going to outperform the market by trying to trade. There are people who chart the price-time relationships of stocks and markets and try to convince the world that they hold the key. If they had the key, then they, and everyone else, would be rich by adopting the chartist systems."

"But, Ang, I remember your saying at times that the market was overvalued or undervalued. How did you account for those conclusions? There must be some way."

"Put yourself in the rational investor's place. He or she wants to maximize the return on investment. Let's say you have $1,000 to put into some financial instrument. What are your choices? In the simplest of terms, you can choose either bonds or stocks. Where today would you get your best return? Well, let's look at the *Globe and Mail* you brought me. It shows Government of Canada bonds yielding 5.5 percent. If you invest $1,000 in bonds, you will receive $55 in earnings each year. Now, remember, the yield is calculated by dividing the income or earnings by the price paid ($55 ÷ $1,000 = 5.5 percent). Let's not stop here. What is the price-earnings ratio, or PE, of this bond?"

"That's a little odd," I said. "I don't usually hear of bonds or loans considered on a price-earnings ratio."

"I am taking this approach so that we can compare the two markets, bonds and stocks, with the same yardstick. To do a proper comparison of shares to bonds, you have to look at what each will earn for its owner. Therefore we are going to look at the earnings of the shares, not their dividend rates. Dividends are the portion of earnings paid to the owners of the company; however, what they actually own is the earnings in total."

"Okay," I said. "The price-earnings ratio is the price divided by the earnings or, in other words, $1,000 ÷ $55. Let's see. That works out to 18.2. So the bond is selling at 18 times earnings."

"Right. Now look in the business section of the newspaper to see what the PE is for the Toronto Stock Exchange 300 Composite Index."

"It is selling at a PE of 24," I said.

"Okay, that means the total price of the TSE 300, divided by the total earnings, gives you a number of 24. We also know from the bond calculation that the reciprocal of the PE is the yield, and the reciprocal of the yield is the PE.

So, in the bond case, the number one divided by the yield gives us the PE (1/.055 = 18.2) and the number one divided by the PE gives us the yield (1/18.2 = .055)."

"Hey, that's a neat little trick."

"That same trick, as you call it, also applies to the TSE 300. Therefore, the earnings yield of the TSE 300 is:

Yield
> = 1/PE
> = 1/24
> = .042 = 4.2 percent

"What that tells me," Ang continued, "is that the investor's $1,000, invested in the stock market, will yield only $42, compared to the $55 he or she would receive in the bond market. So, how can we price the two investments to make them equal? In both cases, the amount of money the investor receives is fixed. He or she gets $42 per $1,000 invested in the share market, or $55 from the same investment in bonds. If we want the investor in the share market to receive the same $55 from the share investment, he or she will have to pay more for it. How much? Look at the three numbers we have to play with: price, earnings, and PE. Previously, we solved for PE with the equation: PE = Price/Earnings. We want to keep the PE equal to 24, and the earnings to come up to $55 to equal the bond cash return. That means we solve for the price:

> Price = Earnings x PE
> Price = $55 x 24 = $1,320

"So, to earn $55 at a 24 times multiple, I have to invest

a third more capital. Let's review the analysis. If I have $1,000 to invest, I can make $42 in the stock market or $55 in the bond market. In looking at price reactions, it is likely that the stock market will come down in price earnings to match the price-earnings ratio of the bond. What does that mean? If I am going to receive $42 annually, and the effective PE is 18.2, then the price potential for the share market is:

Price = Earnings x PE

or

$42 x 18.2 = $764

"Therefore, the investor looking for the best capital gain would expect to see it in the bond market, if share prices are to remain at 24 times earnings on the TSE. Conversely, the investor looking for yield would again choose the bond market, at 5.5 percent, compared to the stock market's yield of 4.2 percent. So either for prospective yield or capital gains, the prudent investor will choose the bond market over the stock market. This will lead to less money flowing into the stock market to drive up prices."

"God, I can't envision bonds with a $1,000 par value selling for more than $1,300!" I said.

"I agree. But in reality it could happen, Stew, if interest rates fell to 4.2 percent, which then implies zero or negative inflation."

"C'mon, you know as well as I do that this will never happen. Let's talk about reality. Something has to be wrong with your numbers or your calculator."

"First, Stew, never say never. There was a time just after the October 1929 crash when deflation was so great it caused U.S. Treasury bills to be sold at a premium, thus providing a negative yield. To answer your question as to what is wrong with the numbers to give a stock-market value that is a third higher than that of the bond market, let's take another look at the numbers.

"It is a pretty simple equation," Ang continued, "with three variables: earnings, price, and yield. We are solving for yield (or reciprocally PE); therefore, we are interested in the only two variable factors, the price and the earnings.

"The price variable is defined in the paper as the value of the TSE 300; only the earnings are questionable. The TSE calculates the PE on the basis of the most recent 12 months or trailing earnings. Investors buy the market on their expectation for future earnings, and everyone gets astounded by current earnings. The astonishment arises because earnings, it seems, are always higher or lower than the experts predict. Trailing earnings are as reported and are therefore fixed, making the PE of the TSE 300 accurate. However, the outlook for earnings is always clouded. But then, as you say, Stew, let's talk reality.

"Currently, as you can see in the paper, the TSE 300 is selling for $9,800 with a PE of 24. That means that last year it earned $408 ($9,800/24). In order for the TSE 300 to have the same PE as that of the bond market (18.2), the TSE would have to earn $538 ($9,800/18.2) next year. A simple calculation, and the result is that in the space of a year the earnings of the companies represented in the TSE 300 would have to increase by 32 percent. Does that fit your boundaries of reality, Stew?"

"I think you've gone over the edge," I said. "I can't think of any economic scenario that could give that type of increase."

"There is one," Angelo said. "That would involve a collapse of inflation and interest rates, leading to a high-flying bond market. In that case, we would see corporate earnings that would not have to be discounted for inflation, complemented by cheap borrowings to finance further expansion. If you recall, these were the conditions that prevailed in Japan during the 1970s and 1980s. These conditions lead to a stock market trading at 70 times earnings on a sustained basis, although in previous decades you could have bought the Japanese market at nine times earnings."

"With these wild valuations, how do you know when to sell or buy?" I asked.

"For that, you would need the Holy Grail or the philosopher's stone. It is the answer everyone is seeking."

"Well, what about you, Ang? You seem to have done pretty well."

"Not as well as I could have, but well enough. I used Bernard Baruch's strategy."

"Come on, Ang, don't be coy. What did Baruch do to make all that money?"

"He always sold just a little too soon. You see, what causes the stock market to really fall in price is when everyone pulls their bids and sellers find prices rolling away, with every trade being done at subsequently lower levels. The person who had a bid in with his broker to buy Bell shares at a half point below the last trade immediately pulls his bid as soon as he sees a major drop in the market. He knows that he can probably buy the shares at three or four points lower. There are therefore no bids as the shares are thrown onto the market. As well as the old adage 'buy low, sell high,' I like 'buy early, sell early.' That way, you avoid the panic at both the entry into and departure from the stock market."

"Angelo, I don't think your PE multiple is going to be a great indicator for when to buy in the market. It doesn't seem to give that early warning signal you're looking for. I remember when the 1990s recession was under way, my friends in the market were commenting that the stock market was selling at about 20 times earnings; however, bond-market PEs were ten times earnings. How do you account for that high multiple when the earnings were going into decline?"

"At the bottom of an earnings cycle, shares trade based on the company's asset value. Obviously, even if Canadian Pacific's earnings are in a slide, its assets are still of some value and those assets can be expected to provide good earnings someday in the future. The price paid for these assets in the stock market will be a function of how long the investors expect to wait before they will receive any benefit, and what the alternative return would be if the same investment were made in the bond market."

"Timing seems to be the big question here. Is there any way around trying to get it right?"

"The only solution I have heard from the pros is to pro-gram buy. This consists of investing the same amount of money in the market at the same time every year. In this way, you will always get the average price. You will never beat the timing problem, but you will never lose to it either.

"Always remember, Stew, that there is no free lunch at the stock exchange. It is better to save your money and invest it for the long term."

"You've been harping on saving money, but so far you have only mentioned not trading; are there other tricks?"

"Yes. To begin with, when you make your annual

contribution to your RRSP, remember that you're not restricted to cash for your contribution. You can also deliver shares or bonds as your contribution. After all, do you believe only your stockbroker can sell securities to your RRSP? First, you purchase shares or bonds in your own name (equivalent to the amount of your contribution), then you pre-register them in the name and address of the RRSP.

"The effect of this is that the shares or bonds are placed in your RRSP with no brokerage or registration fees. Making your RRSP contribution in this manner also allows for some effective tax planning. For example, the brokerage and registration expenses can be used as expenses in your annual tax filing. Further, if you have any capital gains, the share or bond transfer into your RRSP can be shown as a sale to trigger a loss to offset your gains."*

"Wait a minute. What is to stop me from buying a $100 stock and valuing it at $10 when I present it to the trust company? Not only could I build up my RRSP quickly, but I could take a capital loss for tax purposes."

"Now you are thinking like one of us, Stew. Regrettably, the powers that be have already thought of that ploy and most trust companies require that you price shares or

---

* When showing the cost of the securities you purchased for delivery to your RRSP, exclude the commission and use this expense as a charge against current income for tax purposes. The registration fees can also be used to reduce your taxable income. Furthermore, you will probably have paid the higher "ask" price for the securities; however, when pricing them for delivery to your RRSP, use the lower "bid" quotation. This creates a capital loss for the current year's tax filing. You now have three items to charge against current taxes: commission, registration fees, and capital loss.

bonds on the day before you deliver them. However, some will allow up to five days between the pricing and delivery or notification. So, in other words, if you are delivering Bell Canada shares, you have to advise the trust company of the day and price you are using, and, as I say, the date must be within their guidelines. However, one advantage is that you can use the lower 'bid' price at market close rather than the higher 'ask' price. This again saves you money in your RRSP, because less money must now come out of your plan to purchase the shares."

"Ang, is it really worth the trouble?"

"Well, let's say that between commissions and registration fees you lay out $100 every time you trade or contribute. If you had invested that $100 at 10 percent in your RRSP for 20 years, you would end up with a further $673. Now do that five times in a year, every year, and it starts to mount up."

"Hey, Ang, you're talking my language now. We are getting into serious money. Is there more?"

"Sure there is. But remember that you can also make deliveries in the same way when your RRSP receives an interest payment or ends up with a cash balance for any reason. If you buy small dollar amounts of securities, you will pay minimum commission, which is far higher than the calculated commission. Therefore, keep some securities on hand, ready to sell to your RRSP without commission or registration fees on the day that interest payments or dividends are received.

"It is foolish to leave cash in your RRSP as it earns interest at minimal rates. As well, if there were ever a financial problem at your trust company, it would be harder to obtain the cash balance in your account than the securities.

"There's even more. What are you paying as a management, safekeeping, or administration fee to the trust company holding your RRSP?"

"I can't remember, Ang. It's directly withdrawn from the fund at the beginning of the year."

"Just as I thought. That's how most people's fees are paid. The smarter thing to do, Stew, is to pay the fee out of your own pocket and use that expense as a tax deduction in the year paid. That $100 or more each year will be worth a lot of money in twenty years, and you get the tax deduction now, when it's worth most to you."

"Ang, as I understand it, the rules for saving money in my RRSP are as follows:

1. Don't trade. Buy quality and hold it for the duration, if possible.
2. Make my contribution in securities registered in the name of the plan. Always purchase the securities personally and then sell them to my RRSP priced at the most advantageous price I can use, registered in the proper format and without commission.
3. Pay all the costs of my RRSP out of my personal pocket, not out of the fund.
4. Charge the costs of commission, registration, and administration as expenses against my personal income for tax purposes.

"I guess that's it. We've covered all the fine points of the RRSP," I said.

"Not quite, Stew. Have you made your RRSP contribution for this year?"

"No, I have until the end of February to make my contribution and this is only November."

"Yes, but if you had put it in at the beginning of the year at, for example, 10-percent interest rates, you would have already made $1,250, tax free, on a contribution of $12,500 in your RRSP," Ang said.

"Ah, that makes sense. So there's a fifth rule."

5. Make your RRSP contribution, based on your estimated allowable amount for the current taxation year, at the beginning of the year, not at the end of the taxation year.

"But what if I make a mistake and contribute too much?" I asked. "Won't I be penalized?"

"If you determine at tax time that you overpaid for the previous year, you can always claim a refund or have the surplus credited to your next year's contribution," Ang said. "Also, Revenue Canada permits an over-contribution of up to $8,000 before taxing you."

"The only thing that worries me about all this is finding something to invest in for a long time. What did you do?"

"I looked for investments with a good current return that would do better than the stock market."

I thought back to what Ang had told me about markets being efficient and impossible to beat over the long haul. It sounded to me like he was contradicting himself. It was time for clarification.

"Ang, you told me that stock markets were efficient and that nobody beats the market. If that's true, where does the extra wealth come from?" I asked.

"First, the stock-market value grows slightly faster than

the economy over the long term. Therefore, if you buy the shares of a company that participates to a broad extent in the economy, and hold them for a long time, they will appreciate faster than the economy. After all, the gross national product is considerably higher in real terms now than it was 10 or 20 years ago. Companies like Manufacturers Life, Bank of Montreal, and CPR must therefore be bigger, earn more, and hence be more valuable than they were previously. You don't have to 'beat' the market, you just have to participate."

"You're telling me to buy and hold the stock market for the long haul. Is that how you ended up with this lifestyle, through an efficient market?"

"Stew," he said, "I didn't say all markets were efficient. I said that the stock market and some others were efficient. There are inefficient markets."

"This is like pulling teeth, Ang. If there are inefficient markets I'd like to hear about them." I said. "Tell me about it."

"Well, there is the corporate bond market."

"I'm confused. I thought bond markets were very efficient."

"Let me explain, Stew. When I first joined the brokerage business, it was with a big, full-service firm. As the person with the least seniority, I used to have to calculate the firm's liquidity position daily. That involved pricing the inventory. In that inventory were a lot of tag ends of unsold bonds from issues that the firm had done. These were bonds bought from various levels of government, Hydro-Québec, and Ontario Hydro and sold to investing institutions, such as pension funds. I asked the traders at the bond desk the prices for these, and they immediately rattled off various prices based on the current market yields. I noticed that the bid and ask prices were very close. I then asked about some of the bonds of senior corporations that we had in our inventory. The traders phoned around and provided me with the market on each of these, which was the bid and ask price. I noticed that the spread for these senior corporate bonds was much larger. The spreads of $1.25 to $2.50 for these less popular bonds had now grown to spreads of $5 to $10 between the bid and ask prices.

"When I asked about some junior corporate debentures, the spreads were sometimes as much as $50 per bond. There were some companies that had their bonds offered at $620 and bid at $570 for a $1,000 face value bond. I was amazed at the low prices and the huge spreads. I asked a bond trader why these junior corporate bonds were priced so low as to give very high yields.*

"The answer came back in one word: risk. I was told that the junior industrial companies had the threat of possible default, and the bonds were very illiquid because large dollar amounts of the bonds could not be bought or sold. No broker was willing to make a market in these bonds. In other words, no broker wanted to be buying and selling these bonds for his or her own account."

"Then how do junior, or for that matter, senior, industrial companies finance their capital expenditures, Ang?"

---

* Bonds and debentures are always issued at or near par, which is $1,000. When they mature, they will be redeemed at par. After the coupon (interest) rate of a bond has been fixed, any price divergence from par is reflected in the yield to the buyer. Obviously, a buyer of that bond who pays less than par will experience a higher yield than the coupon rate. This is because yield = coupon/price. Since the coupon rate will not vary, any change in price must change the yield.

"A lot of that financing is done by the banks in the form of short-term credit, but you are right: every corporate finance director would like to be able to lock in his cost of capital in the same way you might want to lock in a mortgage rate. This is done by selling bonds or debentures* with a fixed term and a fixed interest rate. These securities require more effort, as compared to shares, on the part of the buyer, who is in fact a lender to the company. He or she must determine if the company has the cash-generating capacity, over the life of the security, to pay the interest, as well as the ability to refund the principal at maturity. With a government security, there is ostensibly no need to do a credit analysis, as this is done by the various bond-rating agencies. The cash-generating capacity of governments is infinite, because they can either tax or print cash. The other advantage for the investor is that there is a very liquid market in government bonds. The stock brokers' bond desks are more than happy to buy and sell as long as there is a spread in the prices, which allows for a profit to be made. They buy at the bid price, which is lower than the ask price. It is sort of like a financial McDonald's with the inventory being bonds rather than fast food. But those same desks are reluctant to buy a corporate bond for their own accounts, not knowing if there is someone to sell to at the end of the day."

"So, Ang, what you are telling me is that bond traders

---

* A bond is a loan secured by a particular asset, while debentures are an obligation on the part of the borrowing corporation to pay interest and principal. Failure on the part of a borrower to pay interest or principal on an outstanding bond will result in the forfeiture of the pledged asset. Should a debenture issuer default, it will be taken into bankruptcy. The terms are often used interchangeably.

actually buy the bonds from their clients and sell to them from their holdings. This differs from the stockbroker who is not really a broker at all, because he or she acts as an agent buying or selling for you and never actually owns the shares."

"Exactly, Stew. That is why inefficient markets develop for some securities. Without a large following of brokers, they become orphans."

"So, you're telling me there are securities out in the market that no one cares about."

"Well, maybe not no one, but certainly very few people. Therefore, without that great mass to determine a realistic price for junior corporate bonds, there is a price set by some trader, somewhere, who has a cursory understanding of what the bond may actually be worth. There used to be a trader at the old firm of Burgess Graham in Toronto who was the market maker in virtually all the junior corporate bonds. Can you believe that? One man called the market on everything from forest products to auto parts manufacturers."

"He must have known a hell of a lot about a lot of businesses," I said.

"No, not really. He kept his spreads wide enough on the bid and ask prices that it was hard for him to lose money on his inventory. As well, he was a great salesman. If you phoned him asking for a particular junior oil bond, you could end up with something in the oil patch quite different from what you asked for."

"I see," I said, "one of the criteria for an inefficient market is that there be only a few players."

"Right. But as well as the inefficiency of the junior corporate market, there is the added thrill of the old-style junk bond market."

"What the heck is that, Ang? Are we talking Michael Milken?"

"No. Milken created bonds that were junk or high risk at the time of issue. Everyone knew they were risky at the time. You had to be aware, from the high interest rates and the other inducements offered to the buyers, that these were not gilt-edged or high-quality bonds. That is not what real junk bonds are about. The real junk bonds were issued as a perfectly good credit but, because of changed circumstances in the company or its industry, the investors began to question their credit worthiness."

"So, Ang, you're saying there have always been junk bonds."

"Yes, Stew. Let me give you an example. Reed Paper of Canada, a wholly owned subsidiary of Reed Paper of the U.K., issued a bond that investors were more than happy with at the time, particularly because of its high coupon rate. However, in the mid-1970s, the investors in the issue began to question Reed's ability to pay its interest and redeem the bonds at maturity. Reed Paper of the U.K. had no publicly traded stock in the Canadian subsidiary, so there was no corporate research on the company to give any indication of how the subsidiary was performing. Now, if there is one embarrassment a bond portfolio manager cannot accept, it is a default. Therefore, with no research to guide investors, and fears about the forest products industry to scare them, there was a general rush for the exit door; in other words, the bond fund managers wanted to sell their bonds. The underwriter, Wood Gundy, which was supposed to call a market in the bond (offer to buy or sell the bonds with a reasonable price spread) decided the risks were too high and refused to purchase large quantities at any price. The bond fund managers turned to the junk dealers and accepted any bid they could find."

"Did the company default?" I asked.

"No. This is where the smart money came in. Reed of Canada was a subsidiary of the Reed Company of the U.K., as I mentioned, and if the subsidiary defaulted on its interest, then the U.K. parent would have lost all its equity in the company to the bond holders. Therefore, one thing you knew for sure was that the majority, and only, shareholder would do all in its power to be sure that the subsidiary company met its financial obligations rather than lose the subsidiary to the bond holders. In time, the forest products industry turned around and the bonds became a valuable property for a while."

"What do you mean by 'for a while,' Ang?"

"Well, this is where I learned my lesson of the 'heartbreak of the high coupon bond.' The Reed Paper bonds were issued with a very high coupon and call* premium. The high coupon made the sale of the bonds easier and the high call premium acted to deter the company from redeeming the bonds early. To get around the high call premium, the underwriters called a special bond holders' meeting at which they proposed that the maturity date† be rolled back to the current date, thus avoiding the redemp-

---

* The issuing company can "call" a bond for redemption by informing the bond holders that it wishes to prepay the principal of the bonds prior to maturity. Usually the company must pay a premium above the $1,000 par value to retire the loan early. This is laid out in the original terms of the loan or prospectus. This extra amount paid for early redemption is termed the call premium.
† This is the date at which the bonds mature and the bond holders must be given back their principal.

tion premium. The majority of the bond holders were speculators who had recently bought the bonds at deep discounts. They therefore agreed to the new maturity date because they could see other opportunities in more liquid securities. The bonds were redeemed at par with some grumbling. However, the smart money that had bought the bonds at a tremendous discount was quite happy to give them up at par early!"

"Tell me, Ang, how do you spot a junk bond?"

"Well, there are several ways, but here are some of the things to look for:

1. It is a bond or debenture issued by a corporation.
2. The company is either poorly followed or ignored by the investment research community.
3. The company or its industry is facing lean times.

"Those are all junior companies and highly risky," I said.

"Wrong. Is Chrysler Credit Finance a junior company? Was Reed of Canada a junior company? How about General Motor Acceptance? All these companies had bonds outstanding that sold at tremendous discounts because, in some people's eyes, they were junk bonds. There was no research available on the companies, and the professional money managers took their usual route when uncertainty enters an investment situation: they sell. No bond portfolio manager wants to be a hero on his or her own. It is better in that business to be wrong with the crowd than right by yourself."

"Okay, smart guy, how do you tell the good junk from the bad junk? Companies fail, you know."

"True, Stew, companies fail. However, remember that

with classic junk — in other words, bonds that were issued as a good credit in the first instance — there had to be enough substance to the company to convince lenders (or in other words, bond buyers) that the enterprise was worthy of the loan. Therefore, in the first instance, the market has already filtered the worthless borrowers from the worthwhile. This reduces the risk of ultimate failure."

"But, Angelo, there is still that risk," I said.

"You are fortunate, Stew. About 15 years ago, research was done in order to quantify that risk. It is in the CFA* readings. As I remember, the article studied the performance of AAA bonds, or the highest-rated bonds, versus B bonds, or the lowest rated bonds, over the period from 1924 to 1964. Over that 40-year period, the B bonds had a yield that was 1.5 percentage points higher than the AAA bonds, but a 4-percent higher default level. So, let's look at that on the basis of a typical 25-year RRSP of $100,000 capital. If the AAA's were yielding 10 percent, the B's would have yielded 11.5 percent. For that average RRSP, the earnings would have been $436,628 higher in the B bonds† and the loss would have been 4 percent of capital, or $4,000. So the investor in the B's would be better off by $432,628. That can make a big difference at retirement time."

"Angelo, that is intriguing because it even covers the period of the Great Depression."

* The term CFA designates a chartered financial analyst. CFAs undertake a three-year study program to learn the analysis of companies, the operation of financial markets, and portfolio management.
† This number is equivalent to the difference between $100,000 at 11.5 percent compounded annually for 25 years, or $1,520,100, and $100,000 at 10 percent compounded annually for 25 years, or $1,083,470.

"Very true, my friend. As well, I gave no value to whatever the bond holders would have received in lieu of their bond principal on the bonds that defaulted. In other words, when the 4 percent failed, the bond holders would have received the company's remaining assets. I included no value for whatever that might be."

"It seems to me," I said, "that the best way to handle an RRSP is to buy some good corporate, some poor corporate, and some classic junk bonds and sit on them."

"If you buy low-grade bonds, you may be obliged to hold them until maturity because of their deep discounts and poor marketability."

"Wait a minute, why would I have to hold until maturity?"

"Let me give you an example. If you had bought a Co-Steel convertible debenture of April 30, 2007, you would have had to buy it at the offered price, which is likely to be $50 above the bid price. If you then decided to sell the bonds immediately, it would cost you $50 per bond. As well, part of the higher yield in these corporate debentures arises from the recapture of the discount from par, which I explained earlier. In other words, every year that you hold a junior corporate, you regain some of the difference between your purchase price and the $1,000 you will receive at redemption."

"Why don't pension funds operate like that?" I asked.

"If that were the case, portfolio managers would come into the office at the beginning of the year, buy a selection of bonds, and retire to Florida for another 51 weeks, seeing as they can't trade. Regrettably, there is the question of monitoring the performance of the companies invested in, and reinvesting the semi-annual interest payments. That is the real guts of the portfolio manager's job.

"Tell me, Stew, as a banker, how do you measure the

credit worthiness of your corporate clients, on earnings or cash flow?"

"On cash flow, of course." I knew what Angelo was getting at. In an annual report, the balance sheet and the income statement occupy the major portion of a novice investor's attention. For those of us who have to determine the ability of the corporation to live or die, the cash flow, or "Uses and Sources of Cash," and "EBITDA"* are the important documents. From those you can tell how much money the company's operations threw off and where else it managed to pick up funds. Obviously, non-recurring items like pension fund withdrawals or asset sales are not going to help keep it alive in the long run. I could see what Ang was getting at. Do a little credit analysis and you can find some winners. But that still left me with an unanswered question.

"Ang, if you do the analysis and it looks like the company is about to turn around, why buy the company's bonds instead of the stock? After all, the bonds, at best, will only be worth $1,000 apiece at redemption, while in a turnaround situation, the shares could soar."

"When?" he asked.

"When what?"

"When will the shares soar?"

"Well, as soon as the market recognizes that the company is doing better," I said.

"Don't count on recognition. Remember van Gogh died before his talent was recognized. While you're waiting for the company to gain this recognition, the bonds will pay you a hefty interest rate. Meanwhile, you are unlikely

---

* "Earnings Before Interest Taxes Depreciation and Amortization."
In other words earnings before non-cash changes and taxes.

to see much in the way of dividends from the common shares. You may have concluded that a company's fortunes are going to improve, but it is unlikely that you will know the timing. There are two parts to the timing: figuring out when the turnaround is going to occur, and knowing when the market will recognize this and pay for it. While you're waiting for both these events, you might as well earn 15 to 25 percent on your money. It is a thesis called 'paid to wait.' After all, your money should be working 24 hours a day, seven days a week. With bonds, it's always working. That is why you get paid the accumulated interest earned by a bond on the day you sell it, even if the interest due date has not yet arrived. You get the interest on a pro rata basis. However, you don't get a pro rata share of the dividends that a share may pay when you sell it."

"You seem to be very negative on dividends in an RRSP. Why is that?"

"Because, Stew, there is a reluctance on the part of corporations to pay dividends* and, when they do, the dividend yields are almost always lower than that same company's bond yields."

"Why is that?"

"It's mainly due to our tax laws, which give favourable treatment to dividends and capital gains. In the first instance, if a company earns a dollar per share, in a perfect market the shares would increase by a dollar each, in that way recognizing the greater shareholder wealth in the company. If a shareholder now sells that share, he or she pays taxes on the capital gain of a dollar per share. This amount

---

* One business mogul stated that "shares are an interest free loan from investors."

of tax is less than the shareholder would have paid had he or she received it as a dividend. Should the shareholder get a dollar dividend and a dollar in interest, the interest payment is taxed at a higher rate than the dividend."

"Angelo, I don't see the point. Your RRSP earnings are tax free," I said.

"That is the point. The investment markets determine the price of securities, and hence yields and capital gains, after taking into account the tax consequences. Investors, placing a higher value on dividends, will bid up the prices of shares, and thereby decrease their yields until their after-tax yield is equivalent to that of a bond. Therefore, preferred shares yield less (though their coupons or prescribed interest rates can be the same) than bonds because their dividends are more valuable to the taxed investor than the interest payment of a bond. You want the highest possible earnings, which means the highest possible yields, in your RRSP because they are untaxed. Therefore, if I told you that XYZ Corp, which was in arrears on its preferred share dividends and whose bonds were deeply discounted, was about to turn around, what would you do?"

"I'd buy the preferred shares for myself and the bonds for my RRSP," I said.

"Perfect marks, Stew. While you're waiting for the market to recognize this fact, your RRSP would be earning money, and you would have the potential to make a capital gain when the dividends are restored. You would have the potential, as well, for some tax-beneficial dividend income. Of course, you would be protected to some extent on the downside."

"I don't like the sounds of that. What do you mean by downside?"

"Obviously, if the situation doesn't pan out, the share price could go down. You might have to take a capital loss, which you could write off against other capital gains in your personal portfolio. In your RRSP, there is no tax relief for capital losses," he said.

"What about the bond price if things turn sour?" I asked.

"The bonds would not likely suffer much, because, as you remember, they still have the asset backing and are paying interest."

"You obviously have given this a lot of thought. It seems to me that the bond market, and particularly the corporate bond market, is the place to be for the RRSP investor."

"Not only the RRSP but also the offshore investor is better served in the bond market than in the share markets. The government takes a withholding tax on dividends paid to foreigners, but allows bond interest to flow out of the country with no tax if the paper was issued for a period of five years or longer."

"That seems odd," I said.

"What do you find odd, Stew? The government in most countries wants to discourage foreigners from owning control of domestic corporations, and so it taxes dividend payments. The world's largest borrowers are governments, so they encourage the holding of bonds by foreigners to finance domestic profligacy."

"If the slapheads in Ottawa were really clever, they would only allow interest on government bonds to be paid without withholding tax," I answered.

"Variations of that theme have been played before, but they caused distortions in the pricing of bonds, and the corporations complained that they were being shut out of the bond market for the government's benefit. So all the interest payments to foreign holders from bonds issued for five years or more are exempt from taxes."

"Why the five-year limit?"

"If there were free access by Canadians to foreign lenders for short-term money, the domestic banks would have to compete for loan business. It would also make the chore of managing the economy that much more difficult for the Department of Finance. As it stands now, the Canadian banks know they have the only game in town, and if you don't borrow short term or mortgage your house with them you have nowhere else to go. As well, if the Bank of Canada changes Canadian interest rates to counter the economic cycle, short-term borrowers and lenders don't have the option of going outside the country."

"Ang, you mentioned that offshore investors prefer the bond market to the share market. Why is that?"

"Many offshore investors are investing tax free. If they want to earn 8 percent, they do so by purchasing a bond with a simple yield of 8 percent. If you, in Canada, want to earn 8 percent, you have to find a financial instrument yielding 16 percent, because you have a silent partner taking half your earnings. Therefore, you have to find something that will gross you 16 percent to net your 8. Your only hope lies in the share markets, where, in doubling your required return, you triple your risk."

"But, Ang, I still get that queasy feeling in my stomach when I think of share prices tripling or quadrupling and me not participating."

"There is a way to overcome that fear, but first let's stroll up to the bodega so I can get some wine."

As I waited for Angelo to find his shore shoes, one thing kept running through my mind. In spite of all the things Angelo had told me, one stood out: "paid to wait." The concept was brilliant in its simplicity. Why had nobody else told me about this? I now understood why many professionally managed pension funds kept the major portion of their funds in fixed-income securities, such as bonds and mortgages. As long as my self-administered pension fund kept making money in fixed income, I was further ahead. There were obviously a number of things that I'd have to keep in mind for my RRSP when I got back to Toronto.

1. Look at the corporate bond section of the paper and make a list of all the deep-discount bonds.
2. Determine what were the circumstances that led to these being low-priced.
3. Isolate those companies that had
   a. a major large shareholder;
   b. "hard" assets such as property, oil, gas, or mineral reserves, or cash; and
   c. cash flow (before interest and taxes) that covered interest expense by at least a factor of three times.
4. Ask my stockbroker why I shouldn't own these companies' debentures, remembering that he or she will give me the conventional wisdom, which will not make me any money.
5. If after due consideration none of the answers can be said to prevail over the long term, buy the bonds or debentures.

CHAPTER 8

Being Thrown
A YIELD CURVE

Angelo had found his docksiders and we were winding our way through the narrow streets. I was still thinking about how boring it would be to no longer pick up the paper in the morning with the hope that the stock market had made my retirement instantaneous. But there were still two things bothering me. I had often seen headlines such as "Bond market rallies" or "Bond market slumps." After what Angelo had told me, it didn't seem likely that the bond market would be subject to wild fluctuations.

I felt that Angelo would probably know about the bond market's fluctuations. Before I could ask, though, we arrived at our destination and Angelo pulled out two one-litre bottles from his pack as we entered.

The building looked like a bar except for the large kegs lining the walls. My host asked for two glasses of Cava, Seco, and put the empty bottles on the counter. One was labelled Montilla, the other Garnatxa. The bartender took the bottles to the vats and filled them while we sipped our pre-lunch champagne. He returned the bottles and handed Ang a slip for 900 pesetas. Roughly $10.

I asked Ang what he was buying — was it rotgut? Ang responded by asking the bartender for a glass of Montilla and another of Garnatxa.

I tried the Montilla, which was about the colour of white wine. To my surprise, I found I was drinking a very fine, dry sherry. Emboldened by this, I changed to the Garnatxa. I could tell from the colour that this was going to be something like a sweet vermouth. I was close. It was a sweet, fruity sherry.

With a goodly collection of potables in front of us, I thought it a good time to get back to the earlier discussions and answer some of my burning questions.

"Ang," I said, "doesn't the bond market fluctuate like the stock market?"

"Yes and no. The prices of short-term bonds,* as a group, do go up and down, but this is determined by what is happening with government-administered interest rates. Obviously, if the government makes cash available and

---

* Short-term bonds are those that were issued some time in the past and are now approaching maturity and hence redemption. The other short-term paper available in the financial markets consists of bills and notes which have been issued at a discount to their face values, for short periods (that is, less than 5 years). These are not referred to as bonds, but as notes.

lowers the central-bank interest rate, there will be a general lowering of interest rates, with short-term rates mirroring the changes. As the time to maturity becomes longer, the effect of a change in short-term rates diminishes. For example, a 30-year bond would probably not be affected at all."

"But what makes the price go up or down?" I asked.

"Interest rates may change, but the coupon rate* on the bond remains fixed. Let's look at an example. If short-term interest rates begin to drop, investors will be willing to pay more for a previously issued high-coupon bond than they would pay for a new issue with a lower coupon. Certainly, you would pay more for a two-year bond or note with a 10-percent coupon rate (or a $100-per-year payment) than you would for a bond or note paying only 5 percent (or a $50-per-year payment). If all the new short-term bonds are being issued with 5-percent coupons, then you will pay a premium for the old, higher coupon bonds, up to the point at which the higher price paid for the older bonds brings the yield down to a level equal to the current yield on the new 5-percent bonds. The antithesis also holds true. During a period of rising administered rates,† the older, low coupon bonds, which are approaching maturity, will fall in price to bring their yields up to match currently available yields."

---

* It is important to keep in mind that the coupon of a bond is the prescribed rate paid, while the yield is the return to the investor.
† Administered rates are those short-term rates set by central banks in an attempt to affect monetary policy. Thus, if the central bank is willing to lend to the country's banking system at low rates, these rates will be passed through the financial system.

"Well, Ang, when you put it that way, that certainly makes sense for changes in short-term rates. But what about changes in long-term rates?.

"Long-term interest rates are a little different. Although governments can influence short-term rates by issuing notes paying more or less than previous short-term issues, their hands are tied with respect to long-term rates. Investors dictate these rates. Over the long-term, an investor or lender wants a real return, or rent for the money, of 3.5 to 4 percent. The investor will then add to this number a premium for risk and expected inflation. Therefore, if in the U.S. coupons are at about 7.5 percent on new government 20-year issues, it can be said that lenders are expecting an inflation rate over the next 20 years of about 3.5 percent (7.5 percent coupon - 4 percent investor required return = 3.5-percent expected inflation). So, as investors perceive a change in the outlook for inflation, the prices they will be willing to pay for long-term bonds will also change."

"So, no matter whether it's a change in long-term or short-term rates, it will still be reflected by a change in bond prices?"

"Yes, that's true. However, to get back to your original question, though bond prices do fluctuate, the price movements in bonds are not of the same magnitude as one would expect to experience in the stock market. For example, a 3-percent drop in bond prices can lead to a 10- to 20-percent drop in share prices."

I was again on a roll and, since we were on the topic of bonds and yields, I decided I would press my luck and try to clear up another area that I found very confusing.

"Ang, what is this 'yield curve' that I so often read about?"

At this point, Angelo asked the bartender for a piece of paper and a pen. This was obviously not going to be a quick and easy answer. Ang sketched out a diagram having two curves. He called the dashed line an "inverted yield curve" and the solid line a "normal yield curve." Thinking I knew a bit about bonds and yields, I asked, "How can you possibly have an inverted yield curve?"

"In order to draw a yield curve, investors plot the yield versus the maturity date, or time left to redemption, of bonds with the same risk rating. This serves as a guide to

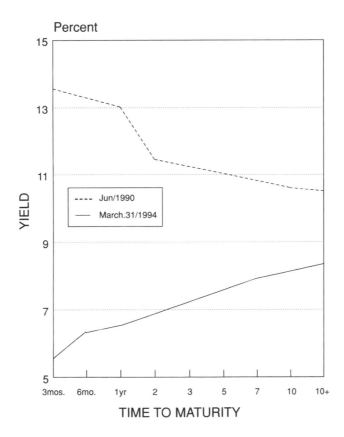

bond purchasing. Normally, you would expect that the interest paid for a short-term loan would be less than the interest paid for a long-term loan, because of the risk inherent in lending over a longer period of time. Wouldn't you agree?"

"Sure. It's a lot easier to predict events over the next six months than over the next 20 years."

"Unfortunately, it's not always that simple. When the government feels that inflation has become a problem, it will increase short-term rates to levels that might exceed long-term rates in order to curtail that inflation. This has a number of effects. It discourages banks from lending long-term money. The banks, by taking deposits, are in fact borrowing in the short-term market to lend in the long-term market. As you can see from the normal yield curve, if you borrow for the short term and lend for the long term, you will make money because of the difference between short- and long-term rates (or the spread, as it is called in the industry). Banks therefore normally pay low rates for deposits, and lend these funds out over longer periods, in the form of mortgages and business loans, at higher rates. However, if the government starts offering higher rates of return, individuals will be more tempted to withdraw their deposits from the bank and purchase government securities, like T-Bills. The banks must then raise their rates to compete. The interest payments on the short-term money may well cost the bank more than the interest they could receive by loaning the money out over the longer term. To compensate for their higher cost of borrowing, the banks will attempt to raise their long-term lending rates. So, you can see we're back to the norm again, with long-term rates exceeding short-term rates. The government has achieved its objective of slowing the economy by choking off credit."

"That seems pretty sensible. But is that all there is to the yield curve?" I asked. "It must look the same year in and year out."

"No, remember that old bogeyman, inflation, is still lurking about. We agreed that over the long haul, investors want 'rent' or interest on their money of about 3.5 to 4 percent. If inflation is running at 4 percent a year, then a bond with a 4-percent interest rate has an effective yield of zero (because what you make in interest is wiped out by the loss in purchasing power). Therefore, investors demand an interest rate that includes the consensus expectation for inflation over the life of the bond. In this case, it would be about 8 percent. New bonds would be issued, paying 8 percent, and old ones would therefore see a price decline to bring them to 8 percent. If the consensus expectation for inflation rates were to fall, investors would be willing to pay a higher price to purchase that same 8-percent bond and a bond rally would be under way."

"Hey, now it's starting to make sense. But don't let me stop you there," I said.

"As I mentioned, governments react to the inflation they have created with the traditional tight money policies, which cause short-term interest rates to rise to levels higher than long-term rates. This produces the inverted yield curve. These inflationary pressures then cause investors to demand higher long-term rates, thus shifting the yield curve upwards, as well as changing its shape."

"Ang, so far so good, but how can investors 'demand' higher interest rates?"

"They do this by refusing to buy the low coupon bonds

at the current prices. Therefore, anyone wishing to sell will be forced to sell at a lower price, which will result in a higher yield to the purchaser."

"I'm beginning to see that there is more to this than half an hour in a Spanish bar can explain," I said. "Is there some easy way to acquire a knowledge of how the bond market works?"

"Probably not, but as long as you understand that bond prices increase when interest rates go down, and vice versa, you are ahead of most Canadians. Understanding all of the intricacies is not important, but if you want to learn more about bonds, I would recommend either *Inside the Yield Book* by Homer and Leibowitz or *The Bond's Revenge*.

"Are they difficult to understand?"

"Only if you can't grasp the concept that yield equals interest paid, divided by price, and that when bond prices fall, yields increase," he said.

I was starting to feel pretty good. We had finished the Montilla and Garnatxa, as well as a Muscat and a dry sherry. It was nine o'clock and time for some dinner for this trooper. I suggested as much and asked for the bill. I handed the bartender about $50 and got back roughly $35 in change. This covered two litres of fortified wine and copious drinks — I had lost count. I thought there might have been a mistake. I figured that the bill should have been twice as much as it was. I nudged Ang, who looked down at the money and demanded another 100 pesetas in change. The bartender recounted the drinks and Ang accepted his tally, realizing we had consumed far more than we remembered. I knew I was in the drinking man's heaven. I wasn't, however, about to be distracted from my quest for answers.

As we walked home, I thought about what Angelo had said.

1. The prices of short-term bonds will go up or down depending on whether administered rates (the rates set by government) are going up or down. The higher the rates go, the lower the prices of the bonds.
2. High long-term interest rates simply reflect high levels of inflation.
3. The bond market is not as complicated as many people make it out to be.
4. The mortal enemy of the bond investor is inflation.

I was curious as to whether or not there was any protection for the bond holder from inflation. Based on my new-found knowledge, I thought the answer lay in long-term high coupon bonds. I suggested this to Angelo.

"Ah, if only it were that simple," he said. "You see, most bonds have that nasty call feature I mentioned to you, but few have a 'put,' or retraction, privilege."

"Hold on," I said. "You're talking stock market stuff now, with 'puts' and 'calls.' I haven't seen an options market in bonds."

"No, but there is what I have always considered an inherent dishonesty in the bond issuer's use of redemption privileges. For example, if you make the mistake of locking in your mortgage for 15 years at 10 percent, and interest rates fall to 4 percent, you can't just pay your banker a small premium and refinance at the new, lower rate. But Ontario Hydro can. If interest rates fall, most issuers will redeem their bonds early, pay the penalty, and refinance at the new, lower rates."

"Hey, that's not so bad," I said. "I wouldn't mind my bonds being called for redemption with a premium, and then buying something else with more capital to invest."

"Sure, you have slightly more capital as a result of the redemption premium, Stew, but remember that you have that because interest rates have fallen. Where are you going to find high-yielding bonds to replace those that have just been called for redemption?"

"Oops. You're right, interest rates would be lower. That doesn't seem fair."

"If you don't think that's fair, look at the other side of the deal. Suppose interest rates go through the roof and the bonds you bought to yield 10 percent have fallen in price because current rates are 20 percent. Can you call up the lender or issuer and say you're going to take a 3-percent discount from the issue price and have him or her buy the bonds back from you? Not bloody likely."

"That's lousy," I said. "You're telling me the issuers can buy back when it's to their advantage, but you can't sell back when it's to your advantage."

"That's right," Ang replied.

As wine-soaked as my mind was, I could still see a gold-plated screwing when it was staring me in the face. I was starting to feel a great distaste for the bond market. As I saw it, the corporation I lent the money to could come and buy the bond back from me if interest rates fell, but I couldn't demand my money back if interest rates went up. What it really came down to was that I could be hurt by inflation, which is what would cause rates to rise in the first place. I said as much to Angelo.

"Wait a minute, Stew. To paraphrase Abraham Lincoln, you can screw some of the people some of the time but you can't screw all the people all the time. You see, if you look at a sheet of bond quotes, you will notice that bond yields are calculated on the basis of the price and the earliest possible redemption date. So, if there is an early redemption feature in a bond, it will be reflected in the price. You should always be sure that the yields being quoted to you are based on that earliest redemption date. Also, when you look at bond price tables, you will see that very low coupon bonds, selling at deep discounts during a time when interest rates are much higher, will inevitably have a lower net yield; in other words, investors prescribe a higher value to them."

"I don't get it, Ang. Why would an investor prescribe a higher value to these bonds?"

"Well, there are three reasons. In the first case, the investor feels secure that a bond with a very low coupon rate is less likely to be redeemed by the issuer. The investor is willing to pay a price premium for this, lowering the effective yield.

"Second, bear in mind that part of that yield is in the form of discount recapture as maturity approaches, because the bond will be redeemed at par. The yield is calculated using current interest rates compounded on that annual recapture. Therefore, even if rates change, the recapture feature continues to compound at the rate prevailing when the bond was bought. Investors like the guaranteed reinvestment rate that deep-discount, low coupon bonds offer, and they are therefore willing to pay more for these, as compared to high coupon bonds. Once again, this has the effect of lowering the yield of these bonds, compared to their higher coupon brethren.

"Third, the portion of the yield made up of discount

recapture is treated as capital gains and not taxed as severely as high coupon interest. Therefore, whenever the sentiment in the bond market changes, it is the long-life, low coupon bonds that see their prices change most dramatically."

Being in the banking business, I knew that there was usually some form of insurance against most risks. Although Ang had reassured me about how I could, to some extent, protect myself from redemption of a good bond, I was still bothered by the prospect of inflation. I knew that as soon as investors let down their guard, the government would go back to watering down the currency to pay its debts, inevitably leading to higher inflation. I asked Ang if there was protection.

"There are two ways to guard against the devaluation of purchasing power that inflation causes. One is to purchase convertible bonds, the other foreign currency bonds. Convertibles are bonds that give the holder the right to exchange his or her bond or debenture for shares, at a specified price. For example, the old Canterra Energy 8.5-percent debentures were convertible at $17 per share, or 58.824 shares per $1,000 debenture. Obviously, if you multiply $17 by 58.824, you get $1,000. However, if the share price moves up to $20 per share, and you multiply this by the 58.824 shares you are permitted to demand, you arrive at $1,176.48. Therefore, if the shares are trading at more than $17, it is worth the effort to buy the debenture, convert it into shares, and sell the shares at a profit. In the above example, the profit would be $176.48 per debenture, assuming the debenture could be purchased at its face, or par, value of $1,000."

"Yeah, but what dummy is going to sell the debenture at par?" I asked.

"Exactly. The debenture price will move up to reflect the underlying share value. In that case, the debenture is said to be 'trading off the stock.' Now, remember our old yield formula. This debenture had an 8.5-percent coupon rate and therefore paid interest of $85 per year. Therefore, with the share price at $20 and the debenture accordingly priced at $1,176, the yield for a new purchaser would fall to 7.23 percent ($85 ÷ $1,176).

"As you know, share prices of companies rich in assets move up in periods of inflation due to the new higher monetary value of the assets. If the corporate assets are in a foreign country with low inflation (for example, companies like Magna or the drug companies and so on, which have operations worldwide) or the company has hard assets (any of the natural-resource companies), the earning power, in the cheaper dollarettes, will go up. This is because revenues are in hard currency, while costs are paid with the inflated cheaper currencies. The increased earning power would lead to the value of the shares underlying the convertible debenture also moving up. The holders of the convertible would now be able to sell their debentures and purchase the higher yielding bonds, now available in the market because of the higher inflation. You are thereby protected from the fifth Horseman of the Apocalypse, inflation."

"It would seem to me that the only safe and equitable debenture would be a convertible. Why don't investors insist on convertibility?"

"The convertible feature is a wonderful option attached to the standard model. But, like optional equipment on a car, it's not free. Convertibles are often issued at a yield lower than what you would expect from a straight debenture. Also, the convertible feature is often included in debentures that might not otherwise sell because of the untried quality of the corporation or issuer."

"Oh, I see: we're back to junk bonds," I said.

"Well, not really. How about George Weston or Noranda? They issued convertibles. Sometimes companies do that as a cheap way of issuing common stock, since they are relatively sure that, sometime before the redemption date of the bond, the underlying share conversion price will make the exchange of the debentures for shares a profitable certainty."

"Very interesting. What about those foreign currency bonds you mentioned?" I said.

"Let's say that you believed the government had decided to throw in the towel on the debt problem. The government would admit defeat, having concluded that it would never be able to pay off the debt without getting thrown out of office. There are only two ways for a government to get rid of debt: pay it off or make it worthless. If the policy makers in Ottawa decide not to pay off the debt but to still get rid of it, then they will use inflation to make the debt worthless. That means that all the precious dollars you have accumulated will lose purchasing power. One of the best lines of defence against this is to buy the currency of a country that abhors inflation. The value of that country's currency will remain constant. In the old days, Switzerland and Germany were such countries. If you were to buy bundles of Swiss francs or German marks, though, you would have to forego any interest and worry about safekeeping. A better alternative today is to buy bonds denominated in Swiss francs or British Pounds. If you look at London's Financial Times newspaper, you will find a listing of bonds in various currencies. Some of these bonds, you will find, are issued by companies or governments with whom you're familiar. It is quite common for companies with assets in a foreign country to keep offsetting liabilities in that country's currency. Because I spend so much time in Europe, I have a portion of my portfolio in English pound bonds issued by General Motors Acceptance and Bombardier Acceptance, finance companies."

Well, my curiosity was pretty well satiated, and we were almost back at the boat, but I still had one minor question.

"Ang, those Canterra convertible debentures you mentioned, are they still around?"

"Sorry, Stew, they last traded at $1,500 per $1,000 bond as the company became the object of a takeover and the shares soared. The takeover is complete."

As I lay in my berth, I tried to put it all together. I was right about one thing. The RRSP had been a big piece of Angelo's escape from indentured service. I was still curious to know what it was worth. I remember his saying that the secret to successful RRSPs was to start early and quit early. So, as a ballpark figure, I speculated that he had started when he was 25 years old. I know he quit at 50, so he had invested for 25 years. Also, he had been investing during the years when a maximum of only $7,500 could be contributed. I guessed that he would have been able to average somewhere between 8 percent and 15 percent on his investments. My reasoning was that if he had bought only provincial government or provincially guaranteed bonds, he was bound to average 8 percent, while his junior corporate bond strategy was likely to provide him with a minimum of 15 percent. I dug down in the bin next to my bunk and found my trusty calculator. I wrote down the following numbers on a napkin from the bodega:

The value of $7,500 annual contributions for 25 years based on various interest rates:

Interest Rate (percent)	Capital Value (dollars)
8	548,000
9	635,000
10	738,000
11	858,000
12	1,000,000
13	1,167,000
14	1,364,000
15	1,596,000

I was astounded. Ang must have had somewhere around three-quarters of a million dollars, minimum, in his RRSP kitty — he would have needed only a return of 10 percent on his money to do this. Achieving this goal did not require rocket scientist intellect; it just required streetcar discipline. As my father used to say, "Strong like bull — smart like streetcar." As long as he never got derailed on his philosophy or contributions, he would inevitably come out a winner. Looking at the numbers, I realized it wouldn't have taken too much for Ang to have a cool million in his RRSP.

It seemed to me that it was time to look at some of those corporate bonds and debentures for my RRSP.

I also liked the sound of the paid-to-wait principle. While the stock jocks were waiting for share prices to double, I was right there with them, but I was collecting interest.

I tried to remember all the things we had discussed, but my wine-sodden brain was having trouble, so I started with basics.

1. Because bonds are issued with a fixed-dollar annual interest payment, any change in the price of the bond will change the effective yield of the bond. Included in that yield is the recapture of discount, or loss of premium, as the bond proceeds to maturity.
2. Watch out for redeemables. There is no use in buying a high yield bond if it is going to be called away from you.
3. Real interest rates are somewhere between 3 and 4 percent, with anything greater being an inflation premium.
4. The government can administer short-term rates, but it is powerless to change long-term rates. These are governed by inflation expectations.
5. The safest bonds for my RRSP are low-coupon, long-term bonds or convertibles.
6. A well-managed bond portfolio can outperform the equity markets over the long haul. This is true because the income flowing into my RRSP is certain, untaxed, and continuous. Any capital gains, although untaxed, are uncertain.
7. I liked the sound of convertibles even though I would likely have to give up some yield. Giving up yield is bad in an RRSP, but I would gain some protection from inflation, which is a comforting feature.
8. It would be important to look carefully at the bond issuer to determine if the company was in dire straits and needed to give away something, if it was an untried company entering the market, or if it was an old-line company doing a stock issue by the "back door."

9. To provide insurance for my portfolio, I would set up a computer program to do an interest-coverage check on each company. I would expect that most full-service brokerage houses could provide an interest-coverage figure.

I started to make some mental notes as the waves rocked me to sleep.

CHAPTER 9

Is There a Doctor
IN THE HOUSE?

I awoke with a big head, a foul-tasting mouth, and a queasy stomach. I was immediately thankful I had paid $10 per day for traveller's health insurance. I was afraid this might be something more serious than the hangover it turned out to be. Angelo looked fine as he sat in the cockpit sipping an espresso. It suddenly struck me that he was probably without health insurance. After all, he wasn't a resident of Canada, so he couldn't have the benefit of a provincial plan. Also, in my province, Ontario, the government had cut off benefits for those who stayed out of the province for any prolonged period, and made it difficult to get reinstated upon return. I wondered how he covered himself for a potential illness.

Sarah brought me a coffee and we exchanged pleas-
antries. I then asked Angelo about health insurance.

"Angelo, what happens if you feel like I do, and it turns
out to be more than a hangover?"

"I go to the doctor," he said, "and I pay for the cost of
the visit. Beyond that, it's covered by my private health
insurance. If I am really sick, my insurance picks up the
first one million dollars of my medical costs."

"That must be expensive," I said.

"It's cheaper than OHIP. I figure that all I really got for
my tax payment of $40,000 per year was the provincial
health plan, given that I sent my kids to private school and
paid for everything else. Compare that to the $3,600* I pay
now — and I am in the high-cost 60-year-old group.
Companies such as A.X.A. Private Patients Plan or I.H.I.
are fighting to keep down hospital costs, as well as their
own. You can have a look at the myriad plans available at
www.globalhealthinsurance.com."

"That seems like a very reasonable price. Why is it so
cheap?"

"Actually, Stew, it's priced at about the same rate as you
pay. The average Canadian in the early '90s paid $11,000
in taxes and consumed $2,200 in health care. So, if there
were a mutual form of private insurance in Canada, the
rates would be somewhat less than $2,200, because only
two-thirds of Canadians pay taxes but all Canadians consume health care. You're probably talking about a $1,500
premium.

---

* Angelo's health insurance covered him anywhere in the world. Had
he chosen to limit his coverage to Europe, his premium would have
been about $1,500 for the year.

"The private plans shave costs because they only cover you for illness, and are not there for day-to-day use. Also, they don't cover all the frills or electives. You can't get a facelift or have your personality rinsed by your friendly psychiatrist on my plan. Have you ever wondered why there are so many psychiatrists in Toronto? It's because the government has guaranteed them an income by paying their patients' fees. There is, therefore, a line-up at the door of your local psychiatrist. The demand for a free product or service is infinite. But very few people have died from lack of psychiatric care. Because of this, the private plans have chosen not to accept this $250,000 cost per doctor, per year. Also, there is tremendous competition in the health insurance field, which tends to keep rates down."

"I never realized that there were private plans out there at such reasonable costs. They must skimp somewhere."

"Not really," Angelo replied. "My plan out of England allows me to receive care anywhere in the world. Let's say I develop skin cancer from all this sunny weather. If I can't get someone to treat my cancer here in Spain, I catch a plane to the U.K. or France.

"Even if you don't come to live in Europe, as a resident Canadian you should start looking into private health insurance. What we are seeing in Canada is a move toward rationing the availability of health services."

"I haven't noticed that," I said. "You can still get treated for whatever ails you."

"Yes, but when? You didn't ask me about my limp when you arrived."

"I just assumed it was something temporary," I said.

"I wish it were. In reality, while visiting an old friend

last spring in Florida, I ruptured my Achilles tendon playing tennis. I had first aid applied at a hospital in Tampa, and then travelled to Toronto specifically for treatment. Sarah insisted on Toronto because my knee had been cared for at Toronto's Orthopaedic and Arthritic Hospital when I tore my cartilage playing squash back in the early '80s. They had all my records and the physician, Peter Welsh, was very competent. I knew things weren't going to go well when, instead of being treated by Dr. Welsh, I was fobbed off onto another doctor. After looking at my ankle and X-rays, this doctor confirmed the damage to the Achilles tendon. I asked him what the course of treatment was for this malady. He prescribed either surgery or casting. When I asked which was the preferred course, he said surgery — and the sooner the better, as the injury would soon be beyond the point that it would be effective. Sarah and I both agreed to the immediate surgery. The doctor left the examining room. Five minutes later, he returned to say that he had changed his mind, and that casting was now the best course of action. This didn't fool Sarah. She asked if this change of treatment was brought on by the lack of facilities. The doctor answered that he couldn't obtain the facilities necessary to operate, and that I should have my ankle placed in a plaster cast immediately. As a result, I now have a limp."

"Angelo, that's a horror story. I haven't heard of other people suffering that sort of treatment. Maybe you were just unlucky."

"I am sure that there are other people in Canada not getting the treatment they should. After all, how would they know whether or not they are receiving the proper care? They have no standards by which to judge the system.

Remember, the health care system buries its mistakes.

"To add insult to my injury, the doctor charged me the higher Ontario Medical Association fee, rather than the Ontario hospital rate, for the treatment. My health plan, which covered all the costs, pointed out that doctors, like plumbers, are open to negotiation — especially in Toronto, where their earnings from OHIP are capped. A cash customer is not part of their earnings ceiling. They said I could have bargained.

"Stew, the deteriorating health care situation should be obvious, what with the closing of hospitals and restrictions on the supply of doctors. I suppose it's better for the government if patients find their services restricted, rather than admit that they are going to be denied treatment. The politicians have already noticed the change and have prepared for it by beefing up their exclusive health system in Ottawa."

I had read most of the popular doomsday books about the hard times ahead for world economies, but this guy was even scarier. He was forecasting capital gains taxes on the sale of principal residences and a creeping withdrawal of medical services. But what Angelo was saying made sense. The future would probably bring two health care systems: a private one for immediate response and a public one with line-ups. Our health care system, which was modelled on the British system, was going to go full circle and end up like the British two-server system. I could see it now. The medical system just over the border in the U.S. already caters to wealthy Canadians. Soon, the poor will be battering down the hospital doors in Canada trying to get in.

I was also surprised to find that good health insurance could be had for such reasonable prices. The difference was that this was real insurance. Most of the insurance you buy is intended to protect you from a catastrophic event that your own finances cannot cover. If you scratch the bumper of your car, you don't run to the insurance company; if a tree falls on it, that's another matter. Then I thought about the name of my plan in Ontario, OHIP, which stands for the Ontario Health Insurance Plan. Originally a form of catastrophe insurance, the plan had evolved into so much more. With Angelo's health plan, he personally covers his day-to-day problems and health maintenance. But should he become seriously ill, he has good coverage and immediate care. It all made such good sense. Mind you, he had better not develop a neurosis or fixation of any sort. But with his lifestyle, I couldn't imagine him needing mental health care.

The thought struck me that, like all private insurance plans, you could be denied coverage or have your policy cancelled. This often happened to dangerous drivers in the private automobile-insurance field. It was a great way to keep them off the streets. Now, with government intervention in automobile insurance, everyone has equal rights to kill or maim you on the road. When I asked Angelo about cancellation, he pointed out that if you applied for care under a U.K. policy, insurance law required that you be treated until your illness was cured or you reached the limit of the liability coverage on your policy, which in Ang's case was one million dollars. As he said, "Have you ever had your car insurer refuse to finish paying the damages on your car from a previous accident, just because you renewed with another carrier, or because the person who caused the accident is no longer insurable or in jail?" Once an insurance liability has been accepted, it has to be discharged.

I also found out from Angelo that European hospitals and doctors have lower fees. In the case of the hospitals, it's because they charge the victims of motor vehicle accidents the full price of their care. This is usually paid by the offending motorist's insurance, thus forcing up auto insurance rates in Europe. There's no subsidized ambulance and emergency care for the victims of Europe's last blood sport. They have to pay full cost for smash-ups.

Also, in Europe, there seems to be some of that old-fashioned reverence for the medical profession. As a result, the "sue 'em and screw 'em" philosophy has not taken over. Either doctors don't screw up in Europe, or their patients accept incompetence or they have no recourse.

I noticed that, so far, we had been talking about Europe only. "Angelo, what about the U.S.? Suppose I decide to move to the States at some point. Won't I have a health insurance problem? I hear health care is murder in the States."

"There are a number of considerations," he said. "When you say that health care costs are 'murder' in the U.S., the question is, compared to what? You'll notice that my health care plan has a higher premium for coverage in North America, not just the U.S. That's because costs in Canada are 'murder' as well, only you don't see them. Sarah is going to require some minor throat surgery, and we priced it at the Cleveland Clinic and the Toronto Hospital. The cost will be about the same in both hospitals; however, in the Canadian hospital, we will be paying with dollarettes, and so the final cost to our insurer will be lower.

"The next issue is the permanency of your move. Most European plans allow you to spend some period of time outside your primary area of coverage and still maintain your protection. These periods range from 30 to 60 days. Other plans allow you to be covered anywhere in the world. My neighbour on the next boat is insured with A.X.A. Private Patients Plan and is covered anywhere in the world. For a lower premium, he could have taken coverage within Europe only, but with the proviso that if he were in North America for less than 30 days, he would be covered for any illness or emergency.

"If you were to move permanently to the States, you might want to purchase your insurance there. The providers expect you to buy your coverage in the state of your residence. In the States, the premium tables of most insurers are based on your zip code. The most expensive zip codes are southern Florida and Los Angeles, which have the highest premium rates. The rules differ from state to state. New York, for example, does not allow the insurer to ask any health questions of the applicant. As a result, deductibles are high, about $4,000 to $5,000 for a typical policy. Other states have different rules and hence different fee schedules."

"What do you mean by a typical policy?" I asked.

"One provider that I am familiar with is PFL Life Insurance, a subsidiary of AEGON, a large Dutch insurer. PFL recently insured a 56-year-old Greek friend of mine moving to the U.S. for $176 per month. He has $3 million of 100-percent coverage, with a one-time deductible of $250."

"Ang, what do you mean by 100-percent coverage?"

"As a kind of user fee, many U.S. insurers pay only a specified portion of your medical bill. So, in some cases, the insurer will only pay 95 percent and in some, 90 percent. As well, they use deductibles to deter frivolous use."

I asked Angelo if health was his only insurance cost, since I suspected that, at his age, life insurance couldn't be cheap. He replied that he no longer had term life insurance because, if he died, there was enough money left to take care of Sarah comfortably for life, and his children would soon be finished college. The boat insurance was costing him about $1,500 per year, and there was a small policy on the personal items he had stored in the U.S.* Ang had been adamant about ensuring that his fixed costs be well defined because of his fixed income. As such, he did not take on any of the fixed costs we do in our typical North American lives. As far as I could see, Angelo's fixed costs consisted of health, boat, and personal-effects insurance, and nothing else.

I asked him about these personal items he had mentioned. He replied that at some point they would stop sailing and establish a life on land, and that items such as pictures, carpets, books, and recordings would bring back an atmosphere of familiarity. He had held on to the really personal effects and had stored them for future use.

The other detail that impressed me was that his private health insurance was competitive. He described to me the myriad features of the various plans he had looked into, as well as their limitations. Besides being able to take your health care anywhere in the world, some of the plans offered air transportation to a country of guaranteed quality care (usually the U.K.) if you were injured or became ill in a Third World country. Your spouse's transportation costs were also provided for, as was a stipend toward living costs while your spouse stayed with you away from your domicile. Some of them even threw in disability coverage.

---

* The personal items were stored in the U.S., in bond, as opposed to Canada, in order to counter any argument by Revenue Canada that Angelo had ties to Canada.

The plans did not want to take on an old liability, unless it was really old. So most plans had a five-year clause regarding past illnesses. Therefore, if you had liver cancer within the past three years, you would have to wait a further two years before you dared to develop it again.

I asked Angelo if he had had occasion to use the plan. He told me that besides his ruptured Achilles tendon, he had developed potential skin-cancer lesions called solar keratoses. These had been removed, and the bills submitted and promptly paid. He explained that as health insurance was an optional expenditure, the purveyors were courteous and competitive.

I was fascinated by this. Being a Canadian and always having had government-supplied health insurance, I had never considered that it could be obtained from private enterprise. But then I had never thought of the concept of private electricity companies, until Ontario Hydro started to look like a bankruptcy case. I figured that this private-health insurance arena must be limited primarily to foreign companies, so I asked Ang if there were any domestic names he knew of.

"What I found before leaving Canada was that there were myriad companies offering supplemental health insurance, but it was designed primarily for the Canadian travelling as a tourist for a limited period. As well, at about $150 per month, these plans were expensive for what they offered. The insurer would cover you for a broken leg or other such injury abroad, but if you took seriously ill they would want you transferred back to Canada. Treatment would then be at the cost of your provincial health plan, rather than at their expense. So if you discovered that you had a brain tumour that required immediate treatment, valuable time would be lost while travel arrangements were made to take you back to Canada. In other words, the majority of domestic insurers offering coverage while outside the Canada are offering accident insurance, pure and simple."

"That doesn't sound very hopeful," I said.

"Stew, wise up. You know we are living in a global village. As we speak, long-distance telephone rates are tumbling before our very eyes. Make some phone calls."

It struck me that, if I left Canada and came back, I could always buy private insurance until I finished fighting out my residency status with the provincial board. Obviously, the loss of government health insurance could not be counted as a reason for remaining in Canada.

Is It Better
IN THE BAHAMAS?

I was more than a little curious about something Angelo had said. He told me that he had established an offshore corporation when he left Canada, and had placed the ownership (but not the possession) of all his assets in the name of the corporation. I could understand the attraction of not owning anything as a way to discourage the avaricious, but certainly there had to be more to it than that. Also, I wanted to know the mechanics of this undertaking.

I asked him if he was acting a little paranoid by taking steps to set up a corporation to stand between him and potential financial problems. He told me about Eddie Gilbert.

Eddie fled the U.S. in the 1950s after having defrauded

some companies under his control of millions of dollars. He went to Brazil because he knew that country would not extradite him to the United States. However, everyone in Brazil, including the government, knew he had taken his ill-gotten millions with him. They proceeded, through legal and illegal methods, to bleed him dry. When they were done, they kicked him out of the country. Had Eddie hidden his money, he might still be there.

Angelo was worried, as well, about what would happen if he went to a country that taxed its residents on their entire, worldwide income. For example, if he moved to the U.S. or returned to Canada, each of these governments would want to tax his income, no matter where or how he earned it. By placing the ownership of all of his assets in the corporation, Ang would be able to legally avoid Canadian taxes until such time as corporate earnings were repatriated to Canada, assuming that Ang did not control the foreign corporation. Angelo might not have had ownership of his wealth, but he did have possession, and that alone provided him with all the security he needed. He could make the rules.

Once Angelo took out all his RRSP money, the funds were no longer considered to be held in trust. As such, he could be taxed on the earnings of those funds if he returned to Canada. To counter this, Angelo effectively put them in trust by placing them with an offshore corporation. If he returned to Canada as a resident, he would have the corporation pay him a small salary, upon which he would be more than willing to pay Canadian taxes. He would have the corporation provide him with a tax-free expense account to cover all his expenses. Revenue Canada would likely not allow the expense account as a deduction against corporate income tax — a concern if he were to receive this expense account from a Canadian corporation. In this case, since the offshore company does not pay any taxes, this would not be an issue. This structure offers substantial tax savings and, as the funds would be beyond the grasp of Revenue Canada, it offers a great deal of comfort and security as well.

It seemed that Ang had thought about every detail — even what was going to happen after he was gone. He went on to make another of his prophecies.

"Most Canadians will be paying inheritance tax, in one form or another, before the end of the decade. You see, Stew, at death, assets are considered to have been sold, and the estate must pay capital gains tax on the difference in acquisition costs versus current costs, irrespective of the rate of inflation. As if this weren't bad enough, most provincial governments also levy a probate fee based on the value of the estate. Therefore, a quasi-inheritance tax is already in place. The very wealthy in Canada use trusts to get around these problems, but the man on the street has neither the funds nor the advice to use these shelters."

Angelo went on to explain his strategy. By providing the trust company with a "letter of wishes," deemed to be effective immediately prior to his death, Angelo ensured that the offshore corporation would effectively transfer his assets to his heirs at death, without taxes or estate fees. How tidy.

The Canadian government allows local and offshore trusts as a tax shield for the wealthy, mostly because there is little it can do to stop their use. Angelo had simply torn a page from the book usually read by the wealthy only.

I asked him about the mechanics of establishing an

offshore corporation. He pointed out that what I wanted was a company in a country allowing bearer shares or their equivalent. That narrowed the field considerably. First, he said, just as a restaurant's success depends on three factors, location, location, and location, so did an offshore corporation's. The potential locations were:

Bahamas	Turks and Caicos Islands	Gibraltar
Hong Kong	Isle of Man	Jersey
Saint Martin	Cayman Islands	Curaçao
Aruba	British Virgin Islands	Panama

How would I choose?

I could see that from a political-stability point of view, Hong Kong and Panama were washouts. Gibraltar might be a bit questionable. The rest of the locales seemed acceptable. Even though there would be no assets left with the offshore corporation, it would be sad to lose the set-up costs to the ambitions of some tinpot despot.

The next question was accessibility, both physical and electronic. Gibraltar, the Isle of Man, and Jersey have reasonable phone communications, but from North America, access is very difficult.

The next factor to consider is secrecy, which is always important when establishing an offshore corporation. The Netherlands Antilles, which consist of the islands of Aruba, Curaçao, and Saint Martin, although practising secrecy, does not have any secrecy legislation; this makes the jurisdiction less desirable than some of the other tax haven jurisdictions. Although my structure would be perfectly legal, it would be important to me, as it was for Angelo, that my private affairs be kept that way: private!

Angelo told me that he had chosen the Turks and Caicos Islands from the remaining options because they are a relatively new offshore finance centre, with state-of-the-art legislation. The Turks and Caicos corporate and bank secrecy, he told me, is second to none. This, combined with the fact that the local currency is the U.S. dollar, makes the Turks and Caicos ideal.

Angelo informed me that the process for setting up an offshore corporation is identical to the regimen here in Canada. One hired the services of a lawyer or a corporation specializing in company formations,* specified the objectives of the company, and arranged the mechanics of the company. The company would then be incorporated and the shares delivered to the holder of choice, which would normally be a trust company. Angelo's specifications were that his company be able to trade and hold securities. Angelo explained to me that most people choose to use different corporate vehicles for different purposes, to ensure that if a particular transaction is challenged, the whole structure isn't jeopardized.

Having determined where his corporation was going to reside, Angelo then went on to write to the corporate formation and trust companies in that jurisdiction to determine the cost of administering the company. He obtained a list of the companies by going on line. The company Angelo chose charges an annual fee, which pays for the handling of the corporation's mail and banking. As well, the company ensures that all filings in the local jurisdiction

---

* One such company in the Turks and Caicos Islands is Liberty Consulting, Box 378, Providenciales, Turks and Caicos Islands, B.W.I.

are done on behalf of the corporation, and provides all of the requisite domiciliary services, such as providing directors, officers, and a registered office.

"Once the directors are in place," Angelo told me, "these individuals then sign the documents to open a bank account, at the bank of your choice, in the company's home base. Some jurisdictions require that a corporation have a bank account in its home country. You can set up a bank account outside of the local area, but banking for a tax haven company in a distant country does delay the transfer of funds and adds some minor difficulties. However, if necessary, it can be done."

In choosing a bank, Angelo told me it was important to make the following inquiries:

1. What are the service charges for issuing and clearing cheques?
2. What clearing services does the bank have available to clear foreign cheques quickly?
3. What are the charges for storage and holding of securities?
4. What are the commissions for the purchase and sale of securities?
5. What banks does it have wire-clearing facilities with?

He told me, as well, that all banks, including domestic ones, like to delay the deposit of funds to your account and speed their withdrawal. During those periods when the money is not in your account, it is earning interest for the bank. Therefore, be sure to reduce the bank's opportunities to keep your funds in limbo.

Angelo conducted his bank research by obtaining the

list of local banks from the chamber of commerce of the Turks and Caicos Islands, and then writing to each of them with the standard list of questions. He used the same procedure to determine which trust company he wanted to hold the bearer shares in his company. He wrote to the various candidates and inquired about their charges and services.

Having concluded which trust company he wanted to hold the company's shares and funds, he proceeded with the incorporation. He cleverly had the corporation open a stock trading account with a local broker. The defining feature of this set-up was that, as a local brokerage, it did not have to abide by all the disclosure rules the big international banks and brokerages currently follow — reputedly doing so to prevent money laundering, but really in aid of the tax collectors. With this account, he was able to trade securities if he wanted to. The local broker opened an account with a large international broker. That broker then issued a funds transfer — restriction letter, which allowed the funds to be paid out to the local broker only and not to the trustees. In that way, Angelo could get paid his interest. Angelo had no position with the company, no signing privileges with the bank, nor did he have any acquaintance with the board of directors. There was nothing to tie him to the company. Angelo gave himself power of attorney over the stock account, and for insurance obtained a letter from the directors allowing him to withdraw all of the cash from the brokerage account. Angelo kept this letter in safekeeping in case of emergency.

Angelo then went on to do something I thought quite logical and clever. He bought some U.S. bonds and registered them with the company; the annual interest covered all the administration costs of the company. This amounted to about $2,000 per year. In looking at the company's activities, he always ignored these bonds. Because the interest paid to the company covered all of the annual fees, Ang didn't have to worry about remembering to pay the annual fee. The other benefit was that he wouldn't have to issue any further payment cheques that could link him to activities in the Turks and Caicos Islands.

Angelo always dealt in bond markets where there was no withholding tax on interest. Many countries, including Canada, have a withholding tax on dividends. Most, however, do not have a withholding tax on bond interest. Angelo explained that he was not competent to judge foreign corporations as investment vehicles, so he stuck with Canadian companies. There is no withholding tax, he reminded me, on Canadian corporate bonds issued for periods of five years or longer.* And it was the length of the *original* life of the bond that was important. Even if he bought a bond that was within a month of redemption, the governing consideration for withholding tax purposes was for how long it had been issued at the outset. There is also no withholding tax on the interest paid by provincial or federal Canadian bonds, no matter how long they are issued for. Many of these, as well as some corporate bonds, have been issued in currencies other than the dollarette. This eliminates some of the credit concerns, since you can buy from familiar issuers in currencies you feel more at ease with. Angelo confided to me that he was in the process of selling his Deutschmark Canadian bonds for

* See Revenue Canada's Interpretation Bulletin IT-361R2.

English-pound Canadian securities.

The only drawback is that the interest rate on these foreign currency bonds is the same as that prevailing for similar credits in the home of the currency. So, in other words, Angelo would be giving up higher-yielding, expensive German currency bonds for cheaper currency, lower-yielding, English ones.

It cost Angelo US$2,000 to set up his company and US$2,000 per year after that for its administration. His annual charge was equivalent to what he would have paid in income taxes on about $3,000 of gross earned income, or the yield at 10 percent on $30,000 of capital. I figured that in my case, I would like to retire on about $65,000 per year net to me. I hoped to retire early, and my strategy was to live off the interest for a number of years without touching the capital. With current tax rates, I would need a gross income of $130,000 a year. Between government waste and deficits, it was obvious that tax rates were bound to go up and my gross income would have to be even higher.

As things currently stood, I had the choice of waiting until I had $650,000 of capital in my RRSP to take offshore using Angelo's methods, or waiting until I had $1.3 million, assuming Canadian tax rates stayed the same — which was unlikely — to keep the capital and maintain my residency in Canada. To get my RRSP capital up to $1.3 million from $650,000 at a 10-percent return would require a further seven years of earnings. So it came down to whether or not I had seven years of my life to give up so that the fat cats in Ottawa could continue to buy themselves privileges and loyalty with my money. It was sort of like getting a seven-year prison sentence. It meant the difference between retiring at 55, when I could still bicycle, play tennis, sail, and hike, or work until I was 62, when all of those abilities might be severely diminished.

Looking at it from another point of view, if I had $650,000 in capital earning $65,000 per year, I would end up with roughly $32,500 of those earnings per year after tax. By moving offshore, my income would go up by 100 percent, to $65,000. Not bad for the cost of a move to some sandy beach.

There were other advantages. The usual practice in Canada was to collapse one's pension savings into a Canadian annuity. Now, seeing as the vendors of the annuities know they have a captive market, you can imagine how competitive they are. Not only that, but because annuities pay out a portion of capital along with the interest earnings, there's the further problem of the capital being eroded. When the government decides to pay off its debts with inflated dollarettes, the annuity takes a major blow to its purchasing power and part of the capital disappears.

Tying up your capital in an annuity also eliminates all of your options. You are locked into one currency and one taxation system. You can count on the fact that the most profligate governments will soon have to severely tax the savings of their frugal constituents. In the U.S., there is a move afoot to tax away Social Security benefits. The Old Age Supplement of those considered wealthy — and at the time of this writing, the Government of Canada considers anyone earning $53,000 to be wealthy — is being taxed away, even though those funds are the property of the pensioners.

I have always been wary of spending any portion of my capital. As such, the idea of parking the money and living off the interest made me more comfortable. Angelo's approach simply made good sense. If you eliminated the problem of taxes, you could park your total capital, retire earlier, and feel more secure.

I asked Angelo how to get going on this.

"Like everything," he said, "the first step is the toughest. You have to either decide to embark on your own or use the services of some of the consultants in the business."

"Hold it, Angelo. What do you mean by consultants?"

"This is a big and growing business. At last assessment, it was the fastest growing business in Canada. Tax rates throughout the world have become so gross that there is an entire industry serving the offshore individual. Whole countries' economies depend on people hiding what is legally theirs from those who would possess it. The advantages of using a consultant are twofold.

"First, you don't have to go through the learning process that I did — or risk making mistakes. Second, by using a consultant, there is less of a paper trail to worry about."

"The one thing that concerns me about your set-up, Ang, is that you have no control over this company that owns all your assets."

"Think back, Stew. Yes, I told you the company owns but, remember, I possess. I have negotiable securities right here on my boat and in my safety deposit box. Most reside in my safety deposit box, because I have passive assets that require little or no attention. With respect to Zeus, it is also a relatively passive organization. It does not require day-to-day management, so there is no need for me to have hands-on control. However, whenever I need something done by Zeus, I need only call the trustees and the company reacts immediately."

"Nothing is without risk," I said. "Where is the potential for a loss with your system?"

"The worst potential disaster is that there could be fraud on the part of my trustees. If that were to happen, I would lose one interest payment on one of my bonds. By then, I would know to change the destination of the interest payments on all my bonds. If I were really concerned about this, I would insure my portfolio."

"This sounds like another one of your three-no-trump bridge bids — thought out to the final play with all the risks covered," I said. "Okay, you've got me interested. How can I proceed?"

"Contact any of the consulting firms such as Liberty if you want help to set up your own little place in the sun. No fuss."

"Wait a minute, Ang. Isn't that illegal?"

"No, Stew. You see, what he does is tell you how to set up an offshore corporation in a tax haven and how to operate it. When and where you take those earnings and how and to which jurisdiction you decide to pay the taxes on the earnings is between you and yourself. You see, Stew, the earnings of the offshore company belong to that company, and are not yours until they are dividended out to you or paid as a fee or salary. You could even set up an offshore corporation simply to protect your funds from the abuses of Revenue Canada,* but maintain your residency in Canada. In this way, if you couldn't or didn't want to leave the country, you could let that kitty grow until you needed some funds, and then pay taxes to Canada at the

---

* For more on that subject read *Tackling the Taxman*.

time of receipt of the money. This is really very much like an RRSP, in that you are saving money until you need it and then paying taxes on it as you withdraw it.*

"Think about it. How would you feel to have an RRSP that cannot be pursued by creditors or the Government of Canada because it is domiciled outside Canada? Then, when you retire, you very dutifully pay taxes on that money as it is received. Everybody lives happily ever after! Where is the criminality in that?

"At no time does the consultant advocate tax evasion. He, like the ads in the newspaper at RRSP time, is advocating tax avoidance, which is very legal. Some of the best practitioners of this pursuit include your elected officials.

"Tax avoidance is one of the fastest growing business in Canada,[†] and will be as long as taxpayers continue to lose faith in the government's honesty with respect to its fiscal policies. How many times have you elected a government that said it would be the one to tackle the fiscal mess, and then been disappointed? The elected have always felt at liberty to disappoint you because they believe you have no alternative but to pay up. Now the alternative is giving birth to a brand new Canadian industry. As a result, Stew, there are a select number of Canadian law firms and accountancy firms that practise in this area and can provide the necessary expertise."

---

* See Revenue Canada's Interpretation Bulletin IT-361R2.

[†] It was taken to its ultimate end when the Tax Act was changed to eliminate all forms of taxation on Paul Martin's offshore shipping empire.

CHAPTER 11

Going Home
WHEREVER THAT WILL BE

My two weeks were quickly coming to a close. I was about to give up the laid-back lifestyle, the food, and the wine, but more than that, the wealth of information in Angelo's head. We had talked about all the practical aspects of his departure, but none of the emotional ones. As with every undertaking, practical or emotional, there is no free lunch. So I broached the subject.

"You can't leave 20 or 30 years of your life without tears," he said. "I mean real tears. As my sons walked out the door of what had been our family home for the last time, I literally wept. But I could see that it was irresponsible and selfish of me to continue to maintain a comfortable lifestyle without making the preparations for the last phase of my life. Did you cry when you first left home, Stew?"

"I guess I did. I see what you're saying, Ang. Change is never easy.

"You know," I continued, "this reminds me of a story my friend Dimitri told me. Most of the Greeks who came to Canada before World War II came from what is now Turkey. They had lived there for thousands of years. When war broke out between Turkey and Greece in the 1920s, the Greeks held the town of Smyrna (now Izmir). Dimitri's uncle Chris was a jeweller, who every morning strolled the beach before breakfast. There he often encountered his cousin Spiros, who was a conductor on the train to Constantinople (now Istanbul). On every occasion, Dimitri's uncle would ask Spiros how close the Turks were to Smyrna. Every time, the distance would diminish. Chris was well aware of the cruelty of the Turks, but he could not bring himself to leave, even though he knew his doom was approaching daily. He died along with the other 100,000 Greeks slaughtered in Smyrna by the Turks."

"Your story parallels my position, Stew. I didn't want Toronto to become my Smyrna."

"Was that your only concern or anguish when you left? What about your friends?" I asked.

"Leaving them was not the trauma I thought it would be. What I learned was that many of the people I classified as friends were only close to me because I satisfied some need of theirs. Once I was no longer available to fulfill their needs, their endearment faded. That was a very traumatic realization for both Sarah and me. This realization and the response we got from people allowed us to reformulate our friendships. We now know who we can depend upon and to what extent. You would be surprised how many of the people with whom you've had the occasional meal turn out to be your fiercest and most unflinching sources of support."

"Don't you get bored being away from your friends and all the action?"

"No. I get much better news here from CNN, the BBC, *The Guardian*, and *The Times*. As you know, we have informed all our friends that we can be reached at our European cell phone number. We changed our mailing address to a forwarder who sends our mail to the different ports of call on our itinerary. My real friends, like you, are always in touch and my days are full."

"How can that be?" I asked. "You don't have a job to keep you interested and active."

"There is a whole leisure class in Canada that, for two generations, has never worked. No, leisure is not boring if you have the intelligence to use it. You don't find a high suicide rate among the leisure classes. Neither the very rich nor the very poor are killing themselves. It's only those who are striving to reach leisure-class status and find their efforts frustrated who resort to suicide."

"Do you ever think of going back?" I asked.

"On occasion. But not to the servitude I experienced before. This world has become such a global village that there is little in North America that can't also be found in Europe. The only thing missing are some of the old ties. Then again, I can go back to visit any time I want. I just have to be careful not to lose my non-resident status."

Angelo, Sarah, and I would soon be going out to a tapas bar for a farewell dinner. I knew that I wouldn't have the ability to grill Angelo further, so I hit him with my last question.

"Do you intend to live like this forever?"

"Oh no! I want to watch my grandchildren grow up and all the rest of it. But where I take up residency is another question. I can still spend six months annually in most jurisdictions without acquiring residency. I might even return to Canada and resume paying taxes, since I am still a Canadian citizen and always will be. However, at this point in my life, I can't make any decisions about where I will end up. That all depends on the tax regime, level of freedom, and quality and availability of health care that each country can provide, as well as a host of other variables."

As usual, Angelo was being rational about the question of where and when. He had achieved flexibility, and he was going to use it for all it was worth.

The tapas bar was owned by a former bullfighter, and his trophies adorned the room. There were bulls' heads, autographed pictures, and all the paraphernalia of this bloody sport. In spite of the decor, I had a wonderful time. The food and wine were excellent. The bar also happened to be a hangout for the crowd from the local marina. People kept stopping by, describing how they had heard from friends by email or via shortwave radio.

I thought about my departure and what awaited me on my return. At home, the government was launching trial balloons in the press about future taxes. Except for the occasional pause, the provincial and federal government deficits were growing out of control, and it was obvious new taxes were on the way. Employment tax levels had been raised to levels where employers were reluctant to hire new workers. Income tax — perhaps more aptly named "working" tax — was so high that people were abandoning the work force. The government was going to have to find ever more novel ways of taxing its people. It was terrifying.

Surely there would be a capital gains tax on housing, and worse, one without interest deductibility. I could ease the pain of this by selling my house at current market prices to a self-owned corporation, thus freezing the capital gain before the legislation was enacted.

The tax-free $100,000 capital gains exemption had disappeared with the 1994 federal budget. I doubted that much could be saved by "closing this loophole" — this last phrase being government doublespeak for anything that benefits the middle class.

Reduce the RRSP deduction? Why not? The only people hurt would be the middle class. After all, pensions for the politicians and the poor are taken care of by the public purse. The wealthy protect themselves from government, and are therefore able to afford a comfortable retirement.

I knew the government would soon look to wealth taxes. If incomes were no longer going up, but asset values were, then it seemed obvious that there would soon be a tax on the assets. The government could accomplish this in a number of ways. There could be annual assessments or luxury taxes. But then, I thought, Ottawa might use the most iniquitous tax of all: inflation. As all these thoughts rushed into my head, I found myself in a cold sweat — and I wasn't even back in Canada yet! I wondered how many other people in Canada spent their evenings worrying about how the government was going to use them to repair the damage wrought by its fiscal follies.

I picked up my wineglass and thought, To hell with it. I was in Spain, the food was good, the company excellent, and the wine superb. I was, for the present, part of the leisure class.

CHAPTER 12

The New
FEAR OF FLYING

··

I was comfortably ensconced in an Air Canada seat on the Paris-Toronto leg of my return trip from Barcelona. I had my laptop in front of me, writing a memo to myself, and trying to think of all I had learned from Angelo. I was having trouble sequencing things, which was being made worse by raucous goings-on in the forward cabin. I asked the steward if there was any way of quieting what seemed to be a rugby team in the forward area of the plane. He replied that it would be easy if these people were, in fact, part of a rugby team. It turned out they were either Canadian senators or members of Parliament returning from a junket, and they were no longer coherent. The steward said I should consider myself lucky, as he had to handle this quite often. He was called upon to serve the VIPs from Ottawa (as he pronounced it, the "P" rhymed with fig) whenever there was a group.

The lady in the seat next to mine spoke up and informed me that she was a journalist. She covered Ottawa and explained that our fellow passengers were MPs from a splinter party that had saved the government from being unseated in a vote of confidence. They had voted, as a group, to support the government on a citizen muzzling law, and had been rewarded with a trip to examine the winter farming techniques in southern Spain, and their applicability to Canada.

I said, "That doesn't make much sense. The climate of Spain in no way compares to that of Canada."

"Don't be stupid. Would you expect them to sell their votes for a trip to examine the North Sea fisheries in November?"

She had a point. She introduced herself as Karen, and recommended we both have a stiff drink to see if it would deaden our hearing. I condescended in my usual temperate manner. While sipping, I thought of what I had learned from Angelo and my noisy fellow passengers up front. He pointed out that the most privileged position you can have in Canada is that of an MP or senator. You get an excellent salary and a tax-free expense account, all for a very short work year. The tax-free expense account is actually just more salary, since all your travel costs in Canada are covered, and you are entitled to cheap meals, cheap haircuts, and a host of other subsidized services. Also, you can establish special facilities for yourself at a time when the general population is suffering cuts in service. As Angelo had said, the priviligentia set up a special health unit on Parliament

Hill to get around those nasty line-ups that others have to endure when wanting free health care.

That made up my mind. I was going to become an MP. But I was no Art Eggleton.* I would never get appointed to a riding by any of the party leaders. With that option closed, I realized that I would have to take a different tack. I concluded that I would follow Angelo's model and make myself a "near" MP. I would remove myself from the clutches of Revenue Canada, give myself a tax-free expense account, and use the money I would have paid in taxes to provide myself with subsidized meals, haircuts, shoe shines — the works. Of course, every true MP also needs the free travel paid for by tax dollars. I would keep the tax dollars and go on junkets to Florence to see if the Duomo was still standing, and whether Renaissance architecture had any applicability for Canada. In the name of multiculturalism, I would take a junket to India to see if the East Indian temples being built in Canada were in keeping with the standards set in Bombay and Delhi. I could see my tax dollars at work, but now they would be working for me.

How did my old, socialist self from university days feel about this? I was going into main-line, heavy-duty tax avoidance. Well, with the rest of the country switching from tax avoidance to evasion, I would look like a saint. At this point, Karen, in the next seat, nudged me.

---

* In the 1993 federal election, the Liberal party leader overturned a locally elected Toronto riding candidate, Tony Prei, in favour of the long-time politician Arthur Eggleton. This process of appointing candidates has become more common at both the provincial and federal levels, necessitating that the quotation "the electorate is never wrong" be amended to, "except during the candidate selection process."

"See, the drink worked. You were away off in space," she said.

"I was thinking about becoming a near MP. I am going to arrange my affairs so that I minimize my taxes and eventually pay nothing to Ottawa. I will then take that money and spend it the same way the MPs do, on my personal pleasures. I am going to take the taxpayer's money, namely mine, and live high on the hog."

"You may not even have to go to the trouble of doing all that wrangling to hold on to your money," she said. "I'm working on a story about a guy from Winnipeg named Gary Hart. From what I understand, he's never paid income tax in 50 years. Hart found that sections 91 and 92 of the *British North America Act* prohibited the federal government from imposing, and hence collecting, a direct tax, such as income tax. That right was left to the provinces. However, Hart found that the federal government obtained permission from the provinces to impose an income tax under the *Income War Tax Act* of 1917. This was the first time the federal government had used the direct taxation right that resided with the provinces. In his research, Hart found that on October 3, 1950, the Supreme Court of Canada ruled in the case of the Lord Nelson Hotel of Halifax* that the provinces could not legally transfer their direct taxation rights to the federal government. The court also ruled that the federal government was to get itself out of all such power-sharing agreements by 1962. I am now trying to find out if the government

---

* Attorney General of Nova Scotia v. Attorney General of Canada and Lord Nelson Hotel Company Ltd.

ever did obtain the right to direct taxation."

"What makes you think they didn't?" I asked.

"Two things. First, the guy who brought me the story claims that Gary Hart was taken to court 22 times and that each time the case was thrown out. In the end, the court told Revenue Canada that if it showed up with Gary Hart again, it would be charged with contempt of court.

"The other consideration is the difficulty involved. As my editor pointed out, if Ottawa gave the direct-taxation right back to the provinces, what is to guarantee that the provinces would turn around and give it back to Ottawa? If the feds even admitted for a moment that the provinces didn't have the right to give them direct taxation, then the provinces would quickly take it back, and the drunks up forward would be out of perks and, probably, a job."

"This sounds like a really interesting story. Where do you go from here?"

"There is an organization out of Winnipeg that has written material on the subject. I've written to the organization to get its package. However, my husband, Frank, ever the pussycat, says I should back off this story. He's afraid I'll get charged with sedition, be harassed, or end up in a *Silkwood** situation."

"I can see his concern," I said. "You are treading on a lot of people's turf here. Money is power. If you take away Ottawa's ability to siphon money out of the economy, you take away its power, and no one ever gives up power readily."

Karen, easily sensing my interest, recommended two

---

* The 1970s movie *Silkwood* chronicled the story of a woman who became suspicious of the events at a nuclear plant, and then died under strange circumstances.

different publications, *Call It Extortion and Taxfighter's Sourcebook,* as well as *The Constitution Acts 1867 to 1982.*

I made a note in my laptop to order the books when I got home. I would charge them off as a business expense, since they would be necessary to reduce my tax load! With my laptop at the ready, I decided to make some notes on what Angelo had told me. I didn't quite know how to prioritize the information. Finally, I concluded that the first element was the RRSP. Here are the important features that Angelo had pointed out:

1. Start early and quit early.
2. Save money in your RRSP by not spending lavishly on trading and registration fees.
3. Buy yield, as much as you safely can.
4. Make contributions in certificate form.
5. Don't leave cash lying fallow in your fund — sop it up with small numbers of securities held for that purpose.*
6. Prepare to take the RRSP out as a lump sum while resident abroad if the RRSP is worth more than $500,000 and the withholding tax rates haven't been increased.

Those thoughts led to others. What would I do with the RRSP once I had removed it? Obviously, the offshore corporation would then be the home. But when should I set up the offshore corporation? The sooner the better?

---

* I have since learned to buy bonds and have small amounts of them registered after their interest payment dates. I don't want to have an interest cheque sent to my RRSP for a bond that has not yet been sold to the fund by me.

That seemed reasonable. As Angelo had pointed out, the cost of the offshore corporation on an annual basis was US$2,000, or the interest on $20,000 in a tax-free environment. Could I afford to set up the offshore corporation, and then park $20,000 in U.S. bonds to pay its annual costs? *The Wall Street Journal's* international edition already had me convinced. It ran a headline story about how the finance minister was contemplating more currency controls in the guise of fighting terrorism to stop the free movement of Canadian funds across borders. I figured I might as well find a consultant and get this done while I was still permitted to take my own money out of the country — and while it was still worth something.

If I earned any income in the offshore corporation, I could let it build up. I could take it out at my leisure and pay tax on it when I actually took possession of it. Angelo was right: the world is a very tumultuous place and you never know when you will need an escape hatch. It seemed like cheap insurance to me to have some money in a distant place. I'll bet there are a lot of folks in what used to be Yugoslavia who have these exact same feelings, belatedly.

I decided to set up an offshore, bearer-share company in the Turks and Caicos. I chose the name Papillon* because it had an aura of freedom about it.

I thought about the steps I would need to take to establish Papillon. First, I would structure the offshore corporation as an investment company that would cover most of my needs. Next, since the idea of the warrant appealed to me, I would instruct my consultant to arrange

---

* *Papillon* is the name of a book, later made into a movie, about a man escaping from Devil's Island.

for the issuance of a warrant by the holder of the shares. When I retired, I would move to a foreign jurisdiction, take out my RRSP with a minimal tax bite, loan all the cash to Papillon at a zero interest rate, and then have the company invest the money in secure undertakings. I would then receive a payment from Papillon and, depending upon how my residence taxed income from abroad, would determine my net income. With all my assets squirrelled away, I would be safe from any strong-arm tactics and able to deal with the taxing authorities on an equitable basis.

I liked this arrangement because it gave me control. With my retirement income in my hands, I could invest in whichever currency I wanted — a right denied me if I left my funds in Canada. I had grave misgivings about the Canadian currency. Although our government is committed to reducing the size of the national debt and its growth rates, there is not the same level of earnestness when it comes to cutting government spending, the source of the deficits. I would have to find a country with a small or falling national debt as a percentage of gross national product, and buy some debentures designated in its currency. I would probably receive a lower yield, but that would be more than compensated for by the expected appreciation of the currency.

Once I had all this in place, I would almost be an MP. I would give myself a pension immediately upon retiring, at an early age. Of course, Papillon would grant me a lavish expense account, paying for my haircuts, meals, medical care, and travel. My pension would therefore need to be very small, entitling me to any and all funds originating in Canada, and I would probably even get my Old Age Security payments.

I knew the liquor I had drunk was taking hold of my senses when I thought of having business cards made up with my name, followed by NMP — Near Member of Parliament. My riding would, of course, be Upper Pork Barrel.

I dozed off to be awakened by Karen. "Get your passport ready and your seat in the upright position. We'll be in Toronto soon," she said.

"My passport is in my travel bag, in the overhead locker. I'll get it after we land."

"No, you'll need it as soon as the doors are open. Immigration will check everyone while on the plane to be sure they have travel documents, and then guard the toilets. Anyone without travel documents will have to go back to Paris."

"What about refugees?" I asked. "Don't they come in automatically?"

"Not without real travel documentation. You see, Air Canada had to ensure that everyone on the plane had travel papers upon embarkation. Without them, a passenger would be unable to board. Seeing as the plane is still in transit, if they find anyone unauthorized on board, the passenger is sent back to Paris, where he or she will have to seek refugee status in France."

"Isn't that sort of draconian?"

"Why? Is there any difference between being a refugee in Paris and being one in Toronto?" she replied. "Refugees are ostensibly fleeing for their lives. They shouldn't care where they find safety. Read the *Toronto Star* and you'd believe that we should admit everyone who has suffered some hardship. Pretty soon the lifeboat will be full, and those fleeing for their lives will have nowhere to go."

"I can see why there would be some concern with

refugees, as they cost Ontario billions every year. But at least immigrants fill the coffers, making up for some of that."

"First, Stew, your number of billions is debatable. I think your calculations are based on the 87,000 refugees in Ontario, costing God-knows-what with their health and legal care, schooling, and prohibition from working. In reality, there are only about 14,000 refugees in Ontario at any one time collecting welfare, and that only amounts to about $700 million a year. However, in addition to the $700 million paid annually by the government, there have been recent cases reported concerning the extended families of Somali warlords, whose two or more wives, living in Toronto, steal $50,000 each from the welfare department. As well, Nigerian refugees have set up a system of forging birth certificates to obtain welfare benefits for non-existent family members. As for immigrants, did you know that, in Ontario, there are 22,000 immigrants on welfare? Let's see. At a minimum of $10,000 per person, per year, that works out to $220 million a year. The combined bill for refugees and immigrants to Ontario is in reality probably just less than a billion dollars, or 10 percent of the annual provincial deficit. You are going to have to get a lot of taxes from the other immigrants to pay for that."

"You must be wrong," I said. "Under our immigration laws, you can't become a charge on the state. Somebody has to guarantee your income."

"That's true. But what has happened is the guarantors have taken a walk, because they are unemployed or they don't want to pick up the tab for their cousins anymore. So what are we going to do? Let them starve? The guarantors know we won't, so they get off scot-free."

"Well, we should kick them out," I said.

"Who should, Stew? The province? It can't, as immigration rests with Ottawa. Now you can see why some of the provinces want out. Even if the federal government was at all interested in helping — and it won't be, because it isn't picking up the tab for the deadbeats — it's too lenient to ever kick anyone out for anything."

"Yeah, well, the criminals are kicked out."

"Only if they get a sentence in excess of ten years. As you know, there isn't much you can do, short of murdering someone, that will get you ten years."

"Damn it, Karen, why doesn't someone do something? Our immigration policy and administration are in chaos."

"The beneficiaries of the chaos ensure its continuance by stifling debate on the subject. If you don't want to discuss a subject, deflect the issue. When the radical feminists were undertaking all sorts of sexist pursuits, they stopped opposition by calling anyone who questioned them sexist. When people began to recognize the atrocities committed against the Palestinians, they were branded as anti-Semitic, although the Arabs are themselves a Semite people. If you dare to question your country's immigration policies, you will be accused of racism by the immigration lawyers and consultants, not to mention the church and social groups. They are all making a good buck out of the chaos."

I was depressed as I sat with my little blue passport clasped in my hands, waiting for the immigration people. I had gone from the elation of being a near MP with unlimited horizons to being the benefactor of all the world's downtrodden. To make things worse, the bar was closed. I couldn't even drink myself out of the funk I was in.

Epilogue

. . . .

It was nearly two years to the day since I had visited Angelo and Sarah in Spain when I saw him walking down King Street in the dull dreariness of November. You couldn't miss him. Who else would be wearing a Greek captain's cap in downtown Toronto? I had spoken to Ang recently and knew he was scheduled to be back in Toronto about this time, but I hadn't expected to bump into him on King Street. After the hellos and how-are-yous, I asked him if he was happy to be back living with the denizens of the frozen North. Ang laughed and told me that he was just passing through.

"Oh, when are you heading back to life aboard the yacht?" I asked.

"End of March."

"That's a long passing-through," I said.

"Well, my business should just about wrap up by the end of March, leaving me just enough time to return to the Mediterranean and resume sailing. I figure most of April will be spent refitting the boat, so I'll hit the ocean at the start of the better, and warmer, weather in May."

I was heading back to the office, but there was much more I wanted to ask my friend. I suggested that we meet at my favourite restaurant, La Fenice, for dinner, since my wife was working late. He, on the other hand, insisted that I join him and Sarah at an apartment in one of the up-market areas of town for a home-cooked meal. I agreed, and we set the time for seven that evening.

The building where he was renting was discreet but substantial. I arrived proffering the traditional bottle of wine and some flowers for Sarah. She still looked great, with her tan mostly preserved. As I looked around, I noticed that the carpets were familiar and the pictures were from Ang's old house. Sarah was apologizing for the aroma of Cuban cigar tobacco that wafted through the place, and I could see a large desktop humidor, which I recognized from Angelo's old desk. I was confident it was full of Monte Cristo Number 2's. My host came down the hall with salutations and asked if he could offer me my favourite sherry. Being an old hand, I asked for a Montilla Fino.

When we were seated, I asked him the yearly question: had he finally returned to live in Canada?

"No, but Sarah and I were both missing our boys and friends. As well, I had let my portfolio management slip over the past couple of years I was away. So we decided to come back for a visit."

"If you're a visitor, how come you have an apartment here?" I asked.

"Oh no, Stew, I don't have an apartment here. This place is rented by an offshore company, and they let me use it when I'm in town."

"The funny thing, though," I said, "is that most of the decorative touches, such as the pictures, carpets, and china, all seem vaguely familiar, like they might have come from your old house."

"Right again, Sherlock. The apartment is mostly furnished with the personal items we didn't sell when we left Canada. We furnished and decorated it, while the offshore company pays the rent, and we have the use of the place."

"Why didn't you rent it in your name?" I asked.

"Caution! First, I was afraid that if I had a domicile in Canada, the government might deem me to be a resident, even though I do not stay here more than the 182 days allowed and meet all the other criteria for non-residency. If I were not a Canadian citizen, I would not have to be as circumspect. The federal government, not surprisingly, would like to have as many names on the income tax rolls as possible. As for owning, if my name or that of an offshore investment company showed up as a new owner on the property tax rolls, there would be a temptation to move that name to the income tax list. This way, neither my name nor that of the investment offshore corporation shows up on any land title documents, so I am pretty well clear of prying eyes.

"Second, if some disagreement should arise between me and some other party, government or private, there are no assets attached or in any other way encumbered.

"Third, as I mentioned before, the tax system distorts

home pricing in Canada so that there is a benefit to the Canadian taxpayer who is a homeowner. This is reflected in the higher prices paid for homes, compared to their pure economic value. Not being a Canadian taxpayer, there is no advantage to me to own a home in Canada."

"Does being a non-resident preclude you from owning a residence, Ang?"

"Not really. There are a number of avenues open to the non-resident who wants to be a property owner in Canada. The foreigner could buy a property in his or her own name, but a safer way would be to use the corporate stance. Remember that York Hanover and Lehndorff were large foreign corporate investors in Canadian real estate, so there is nothing to preclude a small investor from owning property. The disadvantage that you face stems from the fact that owning property through a foreign corporation creates a certain inconvenience when you want to sell. The lawyers hold back 25 percent of the sale's proceeds to ensure that there are no taxes owing to the feds.

"To get around that problem, I have seen people use Canadian corporations to hold real estate. As you know, you can set up a Canadian corporation for about $1,200. There are a number of variations on the theme. Remember that if I were to use a Canadian corporation to own real estate, it would be judged a foreign corporation if I held more than 50 percent of the shares, since I am no longer a resident of Canada. Therefore, the majority of the shares would have to be held by Canadian residents. Some people, to be perfectly safe and eliminate any paper trail, have all the shares owned by Canadians."

"Isn't there some concern, Ang, that these shareholders might take advantage of you?"

"There are three steps to take to cover yourself. One is to have the shareholders of the Canadian corporation sign bearer warrants allowing you to buy their shares from them at a fixed nominal price for a period of ten years. Being bearer warrants, your heirs can exercise them if you should die.

"The second safeguard that people use is to have the Canadian corporation borrow money from the offshore corporation, pledging the real estate as collateral. The Canadian corporation cannot sell the property without first discharging the loan. If the loan to the Canadian corporation is structured correctly, there is no withholding tax on the payments, not even on the interest portion.

"Third, if you don't mind some amount of visibility in the Canadian corporation, you can hold 40 percent of the shares, and provide in the articles of incorporation that none of the assets, representing more than 50 percent of the total, can be sold without the approval of 75 percent of the shareholders. In this way, nothing can be done without your approval.

"The other wonderful feature of putting your house into a company is that ownership can be transferred simply by selling the shares of the corporation. Therefore, if you are dealing with a sophisticated buyer you can change the ownership of the property by selling the shares. The only other necessity is filing a simple notice with your provincial department or ministry responsible for corporate affairs. No legal fees and no transfer fees."

"It seems to me," I said, "that all this is a little excessive."

"If you are the kind of person who leaves $50 bills lying around your house for all and sundry to pick up, or if you have cheap locks on your doors and windows, then the methods I am outlining may seem severe. If you have seen, as I have, the way tax departments tie people's assets in knots through the wholesale use of injunctions and court orders, then these methods seem like a minimal line of defence. People seldom remember that there are two parts to becoming wealthy. The first is to earn the money, and the second is to hold on to it. The nouveau riche are easy pickings for governments because they believe that their ability to earn lasts indefinitely. People who have stopped earning are careful to protect their assets from the avaricious. Therefore, the smart people I have met who insist on owning real estate don't leave it out to be seized by or bartered with a taxman.

"Through the use of corporate vehicles, the ownership of the property is hidden. If an injunction were to be served as the result of a legal dispute between individuals, or between an individual and an institution, the corporation and its shareholders would remain divorced from the legal actions. After all, you can't ask a judge to punish a corporation that is not party to a suit just because its shareholders have issued warrants to the individual being pursued."

"I see," I said, "this is just an extension of your ownership-versus-possession thesis. As you have said, 'Possess anything, own nothing.' It would be safe to assume that it's that friendly corporation of yours that holds the lease on this apartment. But aren't there other ways that Canada can declare you a resident?"

"No. As long as I don't work here, use the provincial health insurance scheme, or develop any permanent ties, I can spend up to 182 days a year here without being declared a resident. I have to be sure to keep all my travel documents, so as to be able to prove that I was not here more than the allotted time. You see, the Department of Citizenship and Immigration will not stamp your Canadian passport when entering or leaving Canada, so it is up to you to prove that you are not in the country more than the 182 days per calendar year. I don't use my Italian passport when entering Canada, as that would mean entering the country as a foreigner, which I am not."

I could see that, as usual, Angelo was doing everything scrupulously and honestly. What bothered me was that he was using the rules against the people who had devised them. I felt uneasy about the way he made such an effort to maintain non-resident status, yet spent almost half a year in the country. Angelo, with his high moral approach to life, certainly should be able to put me at ease.

"Angelo, is this not a sham you're perpetrating, by being here and yet claiming not to be a resident? I know these are the rules, but I feel there is some lack of morality here."

"No," he said. "I really don't reside here, and I don't partake in any of the country's 'free' programs. I like to visit here as a tourist and give the country the benefit of my expenditures. I like the people and their quaint local customs. Does that make me any different from a man who visits Bermuda or Britain for 182 days a year?"

"No, but you are bending the rules," I said.

"Nonsense. Was K.C. Irving* bending the rules? Many

---

* K.C. Irving was one of the richest men in Canada. He moved to Bermuda when the tax regime in Canada became too onerous, and continued to operate his Canadian business empire from there.

people have arranged their residency so as to incur the minimum amount of tax. This is tantamount to your buying a tax shelter, contributing to your RRSP, or selling your portfolio share losers to offset your gains. This only seems devious to you because it's strange and new.

"If you really want to see some bending of the rules, look carefully at the actions of your elected officials. For example, the MPs can, by law, give themselves a tax-free expense account. How about $22,300 per year of tax-free allowance? That is the equivalent of $44,600 a year more in salary, on top of the roughly $70,000 salary they currently provide themselves with and the guaranteed $70,000 per year indexed pension. I wrote to Ottawa on behalf of my old firm to see if there was some avenue for those of us in private enterprise to take a tax-free, unaudited expense account. Not so. There are special rules for the MPs. If you want this to really stick in your craw, remember that the boys and girls in Ottawa have arranged for subsidized services running the gamut from meals to haircuts. So why do they need $22,300 from the taxpayers? Because the rules they write say they can take it."

I knew what Angelo was talking about. The pension alone for someone who spends a term and a half in Ottawa would be worth half a million dollars if you had to buy it.* That made corporate golden parachutes look like peanuts. I remember that, in the good old days, as well as providing the Canadian senators with a juicy, tax-free expense allocation of $10,000 per year, the government gave them 52

---

* If you assume that the ex-MP is going to receive his $70,000 for 20 years and discount those payments back to today, you will find those payments are equivalent to a lump sum of $596,000.

return airplane tickets to their hometowns, per year. I couldn't figure out what they spent their expense accounts on, since everything was already provided. In the end, I concluded that it was just another welfare program for the friends of government.

What really struck me after thinking about Angelo's departure and return was that it was like negotiating a new job. As long as you were on the outside, you could make demands. Once you signed on the dotted line, the deal was struck and renegotiation was out of the question. As long as his assets were unattachable by any government, he could negotiate and make his own rules. Once they had him in the fold — with the attendant ability to seize his assets — it was all over.

Angelo went on to regale me with stories about other tax escapees. One individual sold a major enterprise in Canada, took the payment in the U.S., and reported his capital gain to the Government of Canada. He admitted his indebtedness, but refused to pay. What could the feds do? They couldn't put him in jail because he had not mis-represented his financial situation. They couldn't seize his property, because he didn't own any in Canada. So they just kept sending him threatening letters.

Another individual forgot to pay taxes for a few years until he was bankrupt, and then negotiated a deal to pay off Revenue Canada at ten cents on the dollar. What else could Revcan do? It was better than nothing at all.

Then there was the story of the 1960s anarchist who felt his freedoms were being trod upon by Revenue Canada. For years, he signed his tax form and sent it in with all his receipts. He was obeying the letter of the law by providing Ottawa with all his earnings information, but he never filled out the form or completed the calculations. The worst mistake the revenuers made was to threaten him with prosecution. The anarchist then threatened them with publicity. There is nothing that terrifies Revenue Canada more than the prospect of people finding legal ways of not cooperating.* After much posturing, the authorities admitted that he was complying with the law and continued to compile his tax forms for him. As he put it, if they were going to take his money from him and not give him any say in how it was to be spent, he was not going to assist them. The authorities had to capitulate because he threatened to publicize his methods, which could have become the basis for a tax revolt.

One thing I learned from Angelo was not to fear the tax department, especially if it had nothing to attach. I was so relieved by what I had learned from Angelo that I proceeded on the course outlined by him.

I waited until I saw an advertisement in the business section of the paper, met the consultant in his hotel suite, and had him set up a company for me. He also set up a Delaware company for me and two friends so we could own a powerboat in Florida with a U.S. registration and no taxes.

I could see a lot of uses for the offshore company. I would, as often as possible, cut it in on any special payments. Whenever I changed jobs, I would insist that, since there was no other headhunter or placement firm involved, the placement fee be paid to my offshore company (after the appropriate tax was withheld). I was ready to play the

---

* The Queen's Bench of Manitoba ruled in 1959 that in filing a tax form, a taxpayer need not provide numeric answers in the form, but did need to have records that were accessible to Revenue Canada.

game strictly according to the rules, but whenever there was any room for income allocation, you know who got it.

The greatest benefit I received from Angelo was that I could now see a realistic escape from the system. Prior to our conversations, I would wonder at times how I would ever be able to step off the treadmill. I felt even worse when I could see the ship of state foundering on the rocks of fiscal irresponsibility, while the captain and crew prepared lifeboats for themselves and ignored the paying passengers.

Now I had my own little private lifeboat waiting for me on an island in the sun.

ABOUT THE AUTHOR

....

Alex Doulis was born in Vancouver in 1939 and graduated from the University of British Columbia.

He worked for a number of years as a geologist in Alaska and the Yukon. He was also employed in Utah and Ontario as a mathematician in the early days of computers. His field of endeavour was the application of computers to the analysis of financial problems. He took this experience to the investment industry, where he toiled for 19 years.

While on Bay Street, he was one of the highest-ranked analysts in his field, a partner at Gordon Securities, and a director of McNeil Mantha.

He has spent the past fifteen years living tax free on his yacht in the Mediterranean and travelling.

You may contact the author at his website www.alexdoulis.com or at:

P.O. Box 378
Providenciales, Turks & Caicos Islands
British West Indies